Paris Broke Me (In)

Student Days in France

Kimberly Labor

CreateSpace

CreateSpace Independent Platform
North Charleston, South Carolina, USA

This work is a memoir of late-1970s student days in
France. However, character names have been changed
and many situational details altered in order to protect the
privacy of the innocent and guilty alike.

ISBN-13: 978-1547256006
ISBN-10: 1547256001

Cover image: Rooftops seen from Notre-Dame, Paris –
Sharon Mollerus 2009 – Wikimedia Commons

Cover design: CreateSpace

Printed in the United States of America

4

ஐ Contents ର

Il faut un obstacle nouveau pour un savoir nouveau.
Veille périodiquement à te susciter des obstacles, obstacles
pour lesquels tu vas devoir trouver une parade…
et une nouvelle intelligence.

Henri Michaux, *Poteaux d'angle*

One needs a new obstacle for new knowledge. Try
periodically to create obstacles for yourself, obstacles for
which you must find a response...and a new intelligence.

Paris Broke Me (In)

ಬಿ Part 1 ೞ

The Anguish of Adjustment

1: A propitious beginning—or is it?
16 February 1977

Hotel Raspail. We got in late yesterday afternoon, our six months of study in Pau now tucked securely into memory. I wandered around a bit with Candice in the Latin Quarter, feeling like a country bumpkin fresh from the hinterlands, had dinner in a little Chinese restaurant, and then went to bed exhausted at eleven-thirty.

Apartment-hunting meeting at nine this morning at the hotel with our Paris study directors. I went out at ten with a possible lead. At ten-thirty I rang the bell at an elegant building on rue le Goff, to speak to a Madame Rameau. The room she was renting was on the sixth floor, service entrance, no elevator: very small, white, one dormer window, a bed, shelves, a little dresser, a sink with cold water. Three hundred francs a month. I took it! I've found a place to live in Paris!

Note: ideal location in the heart of the Latin Quarter, near to two large parks, Jardin du Luxembourg and Jardin des Plantes; only 300F a month—we'd been told to count on 600F; very nice family and the possibility of earning money babysitting the kids. What great luck!

After I confirmed the deal, I bought a bouquet of daffodils and went to the Jardin du Luxembourg. Splendid, sunny weather.

17:20 I'm in the Church of the Madeleine. Paris is enormous and overwhelming. I can't absorb everything. I've never seen so much of EVERYTHING in my life.

23:25 I've been listening to everybody's experiences house-hunting and restaurant-frequenting. Priceless: a flat to share with two comedians; a room for 1500F in the sixteenth *arrondissement* across from the Invalides that offers breakfast and evening meal; fights in cafés below other less elegant apartments, with shouts of, "The cops are coming! The cops are coming!"

Talked with Candice, too. She told me about the room she'd found and its distance from the center. "Do you think there's a chance of me isolating myself?" We discussed it, and I felt flattered she should ask my advice.

Tomorrow I move into my little *chambre de bonne* (maid's room).

17 February
I'm completely moved in. There is room for everything and a bit more. It's not as if I were a princess with twenty mink coats. I'm very happy here. Madame even let me take a shower this evening, and their bright red bathroom is outrageous. It's all falling together.

Dinner: I went out to find a restaurant and was chatted up by a Tunisian, a law student. At first not sure, I finally let him accompany me, and he showed me the restaurant area in the Latin Quarter. Incredible: nothing but restaurants and tiny streets packed with students. Shérif had eaten but I was famished, and so we spent a bit of time at Les Balkans. It was packed to overflowing, and everyone looked the same age—between twenty and thirty.

18 February
Distress and pounding heart! I'm not sure I like this Paris after all. This mansard room is completely naked, white, and very small. The boulevards—so wide, so long, so unlike the pleasant quiet streets in Pau. The people, floods of people—it's all too much, too much.

*

I just met my neighbor, Jean-Claude, and he seems kind. I saw his room: he's decorated it and it looks wonderful—and besides, it's a bit bigger than mine, confound it! I hate this white floor. Too much white. Feels like a clinic, or an asylum. Paris is clearly not Pau, and this is decidedly not my room on the rue des Cordeliers.

I'm hungry. I'll go to bed. Tomorrow I'm going to look around a bit for other rooms, just to see what's going; I hope I haven't made a bad mistake.

2: *Becoming international in a hurry*
19 February
What do you know! Everything's fine. I felt awful going to sleep last night—I doubted I would keep

the room because its bare whiteness frightened me. Today I decided that in fact it was too late to change my mind since I'd already paid the first two months' rent, completely moved in, and taken a shower in Madame Rameau's bathroom. And also, I didn't really feel like starting to look all over again.

So I set myself to finding little things to enliven the room, and I can objectively state that now my little dwelling is not bad: a large Indian bedspread on one wall, yellow with trees, flowers, animals; a reproduction of a Cézanne painting; an old map of ancient Europe that I bought on the banks of the Seine; a large Toulouse-Lautrec poster, *Le Moulin Rouge*, also bought on the quays; another large poster showing the sun streaming forth in the forest; and in addition to all this, nineteen of my lovely, lovely post cards, which I've been collecting on all my trips. Regarding the dilapidated table, I took off the ripped felt and completely cleaned the top. I think now with two coats of varnish it will serve quite well. I found an empty old Italian wine bottle on the shelves—left by the Italian who perished here before me—and I'm going to put fresh flowers in it each week. Now still left to find are a pretty rug, shelf paper, another poster, and perhaps some cushions. My trajectory today : Le Bazar de l'Hôtel de Ville—the quays—rue Mouffetard and its superb markets—la Maison pour Tous—and University Restaurant Jean-Calvin, called Châtelet.

About that, by the way, a Parisian *resto-u (restaurant universitaire)* for the first time! I bought a ticket

16

from a student in the lobby. You go up the stairs, turn in the ticket, and get silverware and a table number. You sit down at that table with seven hungry others trying to keep body and soul together, and then a lady comes by and serves the food to the whole table. Not at all like Pau and its buffet-style self-service. Here we're all herded like sheep, and the result is that no one knows anyone else at the table. Nevertheless, the food was good, and all for 3F35, about 65 cents!

I'm wild about my neighborhood—what a lot of life! In the evenings along Boulevard Saint-Michel things are remarkable: crowds of people, boutiques with silk scarves waving, the fabulous Greek restaurants with all their dishes displayed temptingly in the windows, the lights—it's all very exhilarating.

Madame Rameau invited me to breakfast this morning, and when I expressed interest in having another table, she agreed and said she'd pay for it. One thing is clear: she would be pleased if from time to time I'd babysit her kids for her.

Observation: I am living in PARIS!

20 February
Paris is tiring. Got up at ten, a luxury that will not continue once courses have started. I am presently in the Luxembourg Café across from the Luxembourg Gardens, after a day of tourism: exposition of German Romantic painting, stroll through the Tuileries, then a visit to Saint Eustache

Church—I now understand how Ferdinand Oehme could paint his *Cathedral in Winter* the way he did: the height of some churches is absolutely overwhelming!

It is raining. Paris can be marvelous or horrible, spectacular or simply too, too, too much. It's raining *comme les vaches pissent* (as the cows piss), as they say, but unfortunately we are far from countryside here.

Paris is not French. It is cosmopolitan. The number of languages one hears on the street is astounding. Everywhere I'm immediately taken for a foreigner—Scottish or English, which pleases me. A very distinguished-looking Englishman smiled at me as we crossed paths walking near the Orangerie—a smile between compatriots? Funny. Everyone is quite surprised when I tell them I'm American (I admit, of heavily English descent).

The Parisians with whom I've spoken so far are very friendly and helpful. Another myth—that of the nasty Parisian—destroyed.

One sees many students from North Africa and the Middle East, and some of these men look me up and down when I'm out walking and even try to stop me, saying, *"Mademoiselle..."* I just keep walking. I told Shérif, who came by last night, that in all honesty I didn't want to see him anymore. It may be that he's a decent person, but already I can tell that he and I have different interests, and that glint in his eye worries me. Nonetheless, just a moment ago on the street in front of a stationers, I met and chatted with an Algerian, and he was not aggressive or irritating.

The rain has stopped and the sky above the park is blue and pink-gold. It is early evening.

20:00   Oh my soul. That face, and the way he smiled at me. I went for dinner to Les Balkans and found myself at a table where an American family was eating. I didn't let on that I was American, and I felt false and uncomfortable inside.   They thought, I suppose, that I was Scottish or Swedish, or maybe French. As I ate my stuffed peppers, I eavesdropped on their conversation. How clean and well dressed they were. A typical middle-class American family. As I was leaving, the little boy across from me, who had the face of an angel—fresh, wholesome, innocent—smiled a smile at me that destroyed me. I smiled back at him, and then I left. Tears ran down my face as I walked up the boulevard back home.

3: The rollercoaster begins
21 February
12:00, Resto-u Censier.   Unspeakably bad food. This city is *disgusting*.

21:35   All may still be well, in the end.   Resto-u Georges Bernanos this evening—not bad.

Today I bought kitchen utensils and violets for the Italian "vase."   I also got shelf paper and varnish for the table. Madame is truly kind and is going to get me a reading lamp. Tomorrow I'm going to babysit her kids for two hours.

First meeting of "Discover Paris." This is going to be entertaining: we students will follow itineraries and literally discover the city. Every Friday we will recount our experiences.

Poor Anne—she is on the verge of a nervous breakdown. She's still not found a place to live, and she told me she cries at least twice each day these days. She's had the most problems of anyone in the group this year, it seems to me, and I feel sad for her. I'm quite sure that she will rejoice when she's finally back in the USA.

22 February

Alas! Unfortunately, I think that I have made a mistake, an *Erratum*. Above all, let's not panic. But *voilà*, my little finger tells me that this choice of accommodations was NOT good. I knew it before, but it's too late now. The situation: it seems that as I'm being permitted to take three baths a week, I'm also expected to perform certain services, like babysitting. Is my personal hygiene being held hostage? Help! I absolutely must clarify everything with Madame tomorrow, before she leaves for Normandy.

I can just about stand this room, but still I feel painfully homesick for the USA right now, and also for Pau.

Doucement, doucement, un peu de calme, s'il te plaît.

Another Tunisian flirted with me at lunch today.

I feel alone. Will things feel better once classes start? I would really like to have someone to talk to. This city is not for me—alas, that I should realize this so soon!

Patrice, a jet-black student from Ghana on the floor, just knocked at my door. I told him I'd already gone to bed. I feel in a state of fear and mistrust all the time here in Paris. This is not my style! Is it this room, or is it Paris? A place is only as nice as the people whom you know there.

23 February
The Great Adventure and then some! Listen to this: Got up at eight forty-five and went to talk to one of the directors at Reid Hall about my worries. She helped me and calmed me down. Once returned home, I clarified things with Madame Rameau, who, truly, is very nice and not out to exploit me. And she is constantly giving me little things for my room—vases, lamps, tables. I think everything is going to be fine.

Back inside my room, I applied a second coat of varnish to my table, which is really starting to shine beautifully. At noon I went out with Patrice to eat at Châtelet Resto-u, which, remarkably, wasn't at all bad—yoghurt, even. Patrice is acting very nice and I think—without being absolutely sure—that I can trust him.

After lunch he went to the library and I to the Place de la Concorde to walk my itinerary once more. I made a stop as before in the Franklin, the delightful little café I discovered yesterday. Lemonade.

When I got to the Maison de la Radio a strike was in progress, so I decided to come back tomorrow. What to do? I caught a bus to the Centre Pompidou to see this marvelous ultramodern palace of art. This is where the adventure actually begins. Standing in line watching people, I called to a policeman to ask him whether the lines were always so long. After he chatted with me a moment, a girl standing next to me asked me in French, "Aren't you from Provence?" She was blond, small but round, was wearing a bit too much make-up, a purple dress, and green suede boots. Suzel. I ended up spending the entire day with her.

Since the Centre Pompidou line was so horrifically long, we went to call in on a friend of hers, Bernard, in the Marais, third *arrondissement*. Charming apartment, furnished in Normandy style. Bernard is an artist and I saw a few of his paintings—not bad. Alain Delon has apparently bought one of them. He didn't feel like coming out with us.

As we walked back, Suzel explained to me a bit of the history of the Marais, which, apart from the Ile de la Cité, is apparently the oldest part of Paris. We ended up visiting the Centre Pompidou. Marvelous inside! Crazy things. For example, an

22

intriguing—and satirical?—exposition on Woman. Also lots of modern art—Malevich, Kandinsky, Klee.

After this, Suzel and I went back to her apartment in the seventeenth *arrondissement*, right at the outer edge of Paris. She lives with her mother in a flat full of African furnishings. Suzel is only seventeen years old, has already received her *baccalauréat*, and is currently studying and working in journalism. She's a writer, has written collections of poetry which have even been published by a Parisian house. She's working now as a critic for an arts journal. Suzel writes about Bernard's paintings; Patrick, another friend, photographs them; and in this way each of the three benefits thanks to the others. Very clever. As for Suzel's father, he is a television newscaster. They seem to be a rather successful family.

We ate dinner at Suzel's: leek and potato soup, fish, mashed potatoes, cheese. Most everything came out of cans or frozen packages, but it was all good nevertheless. After eating we went out to see a comedy at the *café-théâtre* Court of Miracles. We were late, but it didn't matter much. Suzel ran into friends of hers there, but the place was a smoke bomb and had me sneezing terribly, confound it!

Next we took the *métro* to Saint-Germain-des-Prés, and I treated Suzel to dessert, fancy ice cream sundaes. Afterwards she pointed out to me the ritzy jewelry stores and the funky café frequented by gays and transvestites, the Brasserie Lipp.

Finally it was time to disband. Suzel wanted to take a taxi home, and she dropped me first at my street. She does not seem to lack for cash, this girl. I enjoyed taking a taxi—rare for me, that's for sure. I'm going to call her soon. We are going to see Fellini's *Casanova* when it comes out. I'm exhausted now—to bed.

4: The inevitable entrance of a man onto the scene

24 February

11:30 I can easily understand the attractiveness of drugs: when we're depressed and alone, we want to do whatever it takes to feel better. I say that I understand the phenomenon because, in my case, coffee sometimes acts like a drug on me. Once I've drunk a nice strong coffee and eaten a *flan*—as I did two days ago and as I've just done in my friendly Café Franklin—I always feel a whole lot better. I am presently in the Maison de la Radio waiting for the tour.

23:30 This evening I met Agon. Coming out of the Sainte-Geneviève Library, I was feeling sad and was going to find dinner at Châtelet when I heard someone behind me say, *"Bonsoir!"* I turned to see a pale, thin fellow student type with a leather satchel slung over his shoulder. He had angular features and friendly smiling eyes. We went to Wimpy and talked until nine-thirty. Then we walked around the Latin Quarter and on the Quai Saint-Michel with Notre Dame shining brightly in front of us, he kissed me! We talked about the city in springtime.

He kissed me again, two more times. "Oh no, this can't be true," I said.

We stopped for a drink in a café along the Boulevard Saint-Michel and wrote out our names for each other. "It's true—we never properly introduced ourselves." He is Albanian. He left his country at the age of twenty-one and went first to Yugoslavia and then to France. For four months he had nothing, and he struggled. Finally he began to make it, and now he's studying literature at Paris III.

"You were smiling as I saw you coming out of the library, and I said to myself, 'I'm going to ask that girl to have a coffee with me.'"

"I was smiling?"

"Yes."

In fact, I had been feeling rather desperate, but all that changed when I began to talk with him.

I was quite afraid to begin with, really mistrustful. I explained to him the stories of Shérif and Patrice. Agon said all the right things—he seemed to understand. We talked about absolutely everything, there in the plasticky Wimpy hamburger joint. Politics, communism, independence, the different world views of Arabs and Africans—Agon was sensitive to this, which impressed me—parents, children, men, women, music, so much!

We're going to meet each other in front of the library tomorrow at seven. I really don't know, don't know, don't know…

25 February
With time, everything flees, it all dissolves—Léo Ferré, a sad song.

I met Agon this evening in front of the library. We went down into the Latin Quarter and ate at Les Balkans. Agon also takes a fancy to the big fat waiter who cries, *"Banane à la crème!"* We talked about a number of things. Agon has a large family, three brothers and two sisters, and he is the only one still not married. He plans to marry eventually, for he would like to have children. I told him a bit about my family situation and that my mother was dead.

I'm going to track down a book for him on the rue du Pot de Fer. He will be working tomorrow at his hotel job, which he does every weekend.

We strolled around the sixth *arrondissement* along the Boulevard Saint-Germain. I treated him to a drink since yet again he'd treated me to dinner— he's nuts, too kind. We visited bookstores and record shops. Agon likes jazz and Jimi Hendrix. At eleven o'clock we parted, and he took the *métro* at Odéon to go home to work a bit before bed. He kissed me right in the middle of the Boulevard Saint-Michel in front of a café!! (I'm just not accustomed—)

He left me and I went on home, feeling sad and alone. I don't know what I feel about this boy— this man, of twenty-six years. One of his sisters is twenty, my age.

5: *A strange party in an empty apartment*
26 February

23:00   Another rip-roaring day of adventure in Paris. Went to the Panthéon in the morning after seeking Agon's book without success. At lunchtime I met three fellows who were talking together at my table. One left quickly; the others stayed. Hugo was from La Rochelle and dead broke. Denis gave him a number of addresses to help him out, and his kindness impressed me. After coffee, we three set out for Belleville in the eleventh *arrondissement* to find a special wine that Denis needed for his dinner party. Hugo then took off to find a friend, and Denis and I went to the Opéra. Denis, like me, had never been there. Fabulous building! We decided to go next Wednesday to see a ballet for 10F each. Then he and I walked up and down the wide boulevards, and he discussed his ideas for his party that night and another idea concerning Jewish theater— Denis is Jewish. As we were walking, we suddenly found ourselves in front of the Grevin Museum. "To be seen. Definitely to be seen," pronounced Denis. So we saw it, a very good wax museum with present-day as well as historical personages. I learned a lot about French history, which was satisfying. I seemed to know more than he did, but then he's a medical student.

We went back to his apartment, that is, to his parents' place, which was almost empty, needing furnishing and decorating. He had invited me to his party—a dozen of his friends were coming. As we walked around the empty rooms, he showed me a drawing of his that presented a man falling out of it. It was bizarre, but Denis, too, is bizarre. He made a phone call to a friend and *zut!* The friends thought the party was for next week. Consequently, no party.

Denis played his clarinet for me. What a scene—I will never forget it. A large room with a shiny bare wooden floor, completely empty except for a bed, a big black oval-shaped table, a little desk with a chair, a music stand, and in the corner, a toll house lamp. A large room, mind you. He stood with his back to the wall, playing his clarinet. I stood facing him, near the windows, a busy boulevard far below, and listened to him. It was a strange interlude: he played some very ordinary tunes, but I stood listening very seriously in that empty, half-lit Parisian room.

After this, since the party food was there and ready, he suggested that we eat it. Crazy—we had just eaten! But why not? We sat ourselves down at the black oval table and ate superb sandwiches made of sweet bread and excellent cheese, then some extraordinary Tunisian pastries. Just we two, there in that large, starkly furnished room, with Boulevard Tronchet bustling below. The food was impeccable.

After we finished, we discussed serious subjects, such as the personality. I said that there were certain fundamental things in an individual that never changed: they comprised the essence of that person, and although traits might modify a bit over time, the individual always retained his essential core. One's capricious acts—of course. But the person in all his uniqueness still lurked beneath them all. My thoughts made an impression on Denis.

We decided to go out and so took a walk along the Champs Elysées, strolling also across the Place de la Concorde. I got the uncontrollable giggles.

Denis, on the Obélisque: "What I love about it is the *point*."

An improvised interchange, play-acted by us two:

"Parlez-vous français, Mademoiselle?"

"Oui, mec. Tu veux quelque chose?"

I was dissolving in laughter.

Denis: "It's good, the way you laugh. Me, I can't laugh." I glanced at him and he looked genuinely sad.

We saw the Seine very swollen with recent rain, near to overflowing its banks. He'd never seen that. "Me neither, obviously," I remarked, having been in Paris all of two weeks.

He walked with me all the way to the Luxembourg *métro* station. All of a sudden: "Is there actually *pepper* in this?" I burst into laughter. We're going to meet next Wednesday in front of the Opéra to see the ballet.

I always meet people in the strangest ways!

Backtrack: Just before five in the afternoon as we came out of the Opéra, it hit me that I hadn't yet phoned Agon. *Merde*. I found a drugstore and finally—these drugstores are labyrinthine—found a phone and called him at his hotel. The lady on the other end tried twice to reach him. No answer. He'd already left. Sad, disappointed, I was. So I carried on the explorations with Denis. I'd try Agon again tomorrow. Nevertheless, not being able to reach him caused a hollow pain inside me.

Commentary: Denis, what exactly is he? A boy, a nineteen-year-old kid. And that's very clear. He made me laugh, he was sweet, I enjoyed myself with him. But in the end, he's a mere teenager and not a terribly mature one. He could never satisfy that need that I have deep inside, do you understand? He's a very amiable pal, but that is all.

Agon: he causes something to stir inside me. He impresses me. I admire him, and he's teaching me quite a lot of things. He is strong, but he's gentle, too. He's lived through many experiences. He is a sensitive listener. I let him kiss me, and, I assure you, that is very rare. Nevertheless, I'm not at all sure. Yet I would die of anguish if I couldn't manage to talk to him tomorrow.

6: How to tell whether it's the real McCoy?

27 February

At eleven o'clock I went to a café to call Agon. Success! Until three o'clock, then. At noon Patrice and I ate together at Bullier—terrible, the worst of the *resto-us*, but the only one open. Then we went to Notre Dame Cathedral because I wanted to see if there would be a concert on later, and also because Patrice had never seen the inside. Patrice impresses me more and more. He is a gentleman. He comports himself well. For example, he told me today that he didn't like to eat in the street as you see many people doing, munching on *pains au chocolat* as they walk, little flakes of pastry falling in their wake. He has moral sense. He shares qualities, in fact, with Agon, which shows that people are people, no matter what their color.

Métro to Etoile, then to Bir Hakeim. A moment of panic then, when I couldn't find the street, Jean Rey. Finally, there it was. Three o'clock. Agon and I were reunited! We walked arm in arm. We went to a café and stayed talking for an hour. No subject of conversation is taboo for us. I even told him about my experience with Denis yesterday. For a moment he seemed worried, unsettled, but when I made the observation that Denis was very young and going through a period of searching for his identity, Agon understood—he is very quick— exactly what I wanted to get across: that Denis was too young and not mature enough for me, and that he was not to worry.

About that, by the way: it is remarkable how many things Agon and I can communicate to each other without saying a word. And we gave each other presents today! He gave me an orange. I gave him a pretty postcard showing the springtime through the snow near the Sacré Coeur Basilica.

Telling every detail of our time together spoils it: I will say merely that at four we parted because Agon had to go back to work. He kissed me before we separated and both of us—I could see it clearly in his eyes, and I felt it, too—were mildly starstruck. Things seem to be developing—I am happy to have Agon in my life! We may get together soon at the apartment of one of his friends. I said that I'd really like to cook for him. The friend would give us the use of his studio for the entire evening. Just the two of us...

After I left Agon today, I visited the Eiffel Tower and then went back to Notre Dame for an organ concert of Mozart, Bach, and Vivaldi. Very beautiful. A well-spent hour. Ate dinner at Les Balkans. Seven francs for the *poulet aux riz sauce tomate*.

Walked back home. The jerks of all stripes in the street don't hassle me as much as before, and when they do I don't let them get to me. Let them mutter their stupidities. "Hi, how are you?" *"Tu ne cherches pas un copain?"* I ignore, I walk on, with my face set in a Paris-acquired mask of steely indifference. *Moi*, I have my friend, my *copain*.

21:00 The life of a poor student in the Big City: there are worse catastrophes in this world than being obliged to bathe without a bathtub and with only cold water. Welcome to the world, oh you young *bourgeoise*! Nevertheless (she adds humbly), I hope that this sort of necessity will not arise often.

28 February
8:30 What is it, this "love"? I don't know. I think I've never known it. I have a sinking feeling that things are not going to work out with Agon. Not the real thing. Oh it pains me, but why lie to myself? I'll see him at eight-thirty tonight. One can have sudden instincts, but oh how true it is that one cannot see the forest for the trees, alas. What I don't like, what I'm tired of, is being obliged to meet him in cafés and restaurants. How impersonal this becomes after a while.

14:30 Good afternoon. It is raining and beastly cold. Filthy weather. I am waiting for a course to begin here in the Milne Edwards Amphitheatre, Sorbonne. I attended two courses this morning: the Renaissance in France with Professor Bertrand, who seems marvelous; and Modern History: the French Revolution with a curious gentleman, very emphatic, pompous, but amusing at the same time. I talked with him after class, as we both happened to be taking the same bus, and he said he gave lectures at UCLA, USC, and Oxford. His sole subject was the French Revolution. I'm not going to take his course, having already studied this subject quite thoroughly back at UCLA with dear old Symcox. The Renaissance course looks interesting, however.

23:00 I keep thinking about Agon. At Châtelet while I was selling one of my *resto-u* tickets to another poor soul, I turned around and there he was. We each had freshly washed heads of hair. We dined at a ridiculously fast pace, unfortunately, like kennel dogs at feed time, and then we went to a café where we drank kirs. They were delicious—blackcurrant liqueur topped with white wine. He is so sweet, this Agon. I showed him my slides of Pau, and he showed me a photo of a Yugoslavian village on the sea coast, very beautiful.

He seems to like me quite a lot. But sometimes I have no confidence in myself, and I wonder how a man could ever love me. I am too thin; I've lost weight since I've been in France. And my complexion is not perfect.

"I will go back to the USA probably in August."

"Unless you get married here."

"Oh yes," I say, only half-seriously. "It's always possible, one never knows." I laugh, I smile, and he smiles at me, too. As Fleur wrote in her letter concerning her *amour*, "How many messages there are in his eyes!"

It is possible that in spite of myself and my deepest feelings, once I get used to a person I begin easily to depend upon him. Of course it is simply good to have a friend in a large city, and Agon is not pressuring me in any way.

7: *Long unpredictable days and ruminations on love*

3 March

0:30 It's about time a halt was called to this: every night I find myself getting home at midnight. Last night I met Agon at a café after his exam and our conversation went on forever. Tonight I met Denis at the Opéra, a very good program of ballet, choreographed by Jerome Robbins and Maurice Béjart and others. At last I got to see *The Rite of Spring:* superb piece and the music is mesmerizing. The Opéra dancers were very strong, impressive. For 10F (student price) we were seated in the very first row! It is remarkable, however, how much nicer it is to be with someone we really like than with someone about whom we feel indifferently, in spite of pleasant circumstances. The ballet was beautiful, but Denis is not in the least bit like Agon, not in the least.

4 March

0:30   Agon and I had dinner in a reasonable little restaurant on the rue Mouffetard. We took a walk afterwards, and at the Place Saint-Michel we ran into Mouna, who was holding forth to a crowd of people. We stopped to listen to him for a moment—remarkable, exactly like the grizzled old prophet who pilgrimages through Westwood Village in Los Angeles from time to time.

Earlier, I'd paid a visit to the Louvre with an art course, then walked my itinerary in the very pleasant sixth *arrondissement* under sunny skies. I saw a student demonstration (wasn't sure of their grievance), bought a book from a very nice fellow along Saint-Michel, and chatted with a Tunisian student.

Went to the Base Course and then at eight-thirty met Agon at Censier *métro*. I have to say it: I'm not in love. Full stop. What a pity! I think I've never, in all my short life, been truly, truly in love. Perhaps I don't know what it is, this *in love*. I imagine that it has to do with passion, a bit of craziness even, with a deep understanding between the two, with a bonding of the spirit so closely it is as if the two were one person, with an instinctive sort of communication and a very finely tuned sensitivity between the two. But in the end I haven't a clue.

I felt love today in the park on the Ile de la Cité. I was watching two kids playing and two very old people, a man and a woman, talking on a bench. I felt full of love, of warmth, of joy. And I was all alone, with my little notebook. But I am still curious. Love: isn't it a searing flame, an exquisite interior passion, a sort of ecstasy? Well, whatever I may write or say in the coming days, I will leave written in ink here, on this page, that although I like him and appreciate the companionship, I am not in love with Agon.

20:00   Just had dinner at Châtelet (the most passable *resto-u* city-wide, I think I can state). I have definitely lost weight—I am now truly thin. But I like this city; so what if I'm often hungry. I'm an historian-in-the-making and happy to be so!

I am in the Sainte-Geneviève Library. There aren't too many people here, and there is no noise. The architecture is admirable: I love everything ancient and atmospheric. In looking around me I see that the majority of readers are men, not women. Across from me is an American, I think: he has a French-English dictionary and an American look about him.

This is what I've chosen for my courses this semester:
1. Base Course on Paris (required)
2. French Art History 1900-1945
3. French Renaissance, Sixteenth Century
My courses seem good and not liable to burden me with too much work so that, happily, I can enjoy myself and see a lot of Paris.

Anne and I had a good discussion today as we meandered from class to lunch to a café and back to her room (one found at last!) on the rue de la Harpe. We talked about everything, including that phantom love. She says she's touched it but has lived without it for long periods of time, like me.

I'm wondering what the guy across from me is reading.

23:50 The American I spoke of earlier: I met him and we had a long conversation in a café near the library. A rather extraordinary guy. He made me realize how little I really know about the world around me. He was about thirty, hailed from Boston, and had worked as a lawyer for five years in the USA. Shivering, he left Boston to go to Mexico. From there, to Peru and Argentina and then to Brazil. Next he went to Spain and Italy, and finally here he is in France. He's currently perfecting his French and living with a female friend. Everywhere he's traveled he's stayed with friends. He is *débrouillard*. He's very knowledgeable about politics, world affairs, Latin American history, and he speaks fluent Spanish. He is very intelligent, with a critical mind. We talked for an hour and a quarter, and during this time I realized that I had *so much* still to learn about: the revolution in Chile, Ford's foreign policies, the war in the Middle East. And quite a lot else. I also realized that education in the USA is not necessarily inferior to education in France, for this was a very accomplished gentleman.

He doesn't like to go home in the evenings because his friend is currently interested in a guy whom he cannot stand. I told him I'd invite him over to my place if my room were not the size of a packet of Gauloises. Maybe we'd see each other in the library, we said. He works quite a lot in there these days. So we said good-bye.

"What's your name?" He was already on the other side of the street.

"Peter. Yours?"

"Josie."

Always a good idea before leaving a person to learn their first name!

Paris is fantastic: so many different, stimulating people, each with such special qualities. What luck I have to be here. Tomorrow I begin to *read*. As Peter said, someone who studies independently is always more motivated and serious than someone who simply takes a ready-made academic course. I will do both! *Allez!*

8: *Are Paris and I really meant for each other?*
5 March
16:55   Sainte-Geneviève again. The bureaucracy in this library is frightful. I have never in my life witnessed so many useless and completely inane procedures concerning books! A pile of cards to fill out and ridiculously long waits. The French,

when it comes to organization, are out of their minds!

6 March
1:00   Well after midnight. This has *got* to stop. Folies Bergères this evening with Anne. Total decadence, very trite. The subject does not merit discussion. Exhausted, I am, with a sore throat. This is the end of my late-night adventures.

10:50   I feel alone and sad at this moment. I'm a bit sick, and I just read an article in the *Nouvel Obs* about a woman's experience with cancer. That made me think about my dear mother, who died two years ago of leukemia. I'm thinking also of Agon and would like to see him, but I know that first of all, he's working, and secondly, I too have work to do and shouldn't go out with this cold. Also in my thoughts: this is certainly no luxury room; Paris is so incredibly huge; having read all the articles in my magazine about film and theater, I see that I am very unlettered. Sundry reflections of a Sunday morning.

12:30   It is true that I can be quite clever: despite the extremely small size of this room, I have conceived a method for hanging up laundry to dry here. Everything is possible in this world.

18:35   I saw him, we had a drink, we talked, and now I can discern some meaning in the world. Oh how indispensable it is to have a friend! To recap: When my telephone call was cut off this afternoon, I renounced the whole business for two hours and went to a museum. Agon later told me that they'd let him know at the hotel that an American had tried to contact him but that they'd lost the connection. He said that this had thrown him into a state of worry and that he was very happy when I called back. This made *me* happy! We are going to go to the theater one day soon. I will see him next Wednesday evening at seven at the Saint-Michel fountain. Our friendship becomes stronger each time we see each other.

7 March

22:00 I cannot believe how quickly time is passing. Already I've been in Paris for more than three weeks. However, I am in fact sick. *Zut alors!* But I shall carry on despite this throat and this aching head. It's all my late-night comings-home, and the *resto-us*.

It may be that this city is beautiful and full of nice surprises, but it also can feel very big, ugly, and impersonal. Thank God I have Agon. If I didn't have a friend in this vast metropolis, I would be truly desperate. Paris is so overwhelming that in spite of my efforts, I will never succeed in getting to know it. Four months—that's nothing at all. I will never be anything but a tourist here, a foreigner. Pau: I knew it well and it became my home. Paris so far is still very unfamiliar to me and sometimes even frightening. I cried today in the *métro* as I waited for the train. *Filthy, filthy city*, I thought.

8 March

18:00   Observations and thoughts, seated in a café at the intersection of Boulevards Raspail and Montparnasse.   I will never live permanently in France.   The little French children carry far too many books in packs on their backs—stupid and excessive, especially for their age!   I do not like the Big City.   The people who pass hurriedly in the street before me, in front of this café, do not look good.   I'm not making any inferences about their characters   or   personalities.   I'm   simply commenting on their physical aspect.   They look pinched and harassed.   One good thing: except for some rotund aged men and ladies, most everyone you see here is very slim.

I feel bored.   I am wondering whether my point of view would be different if my lodgings were different.   I who was so passionate about *culture* back in Los Angeles now find myself feeling rather *blasée*.   Oh yes, I continue to go to museums, plays, and concerts, but all of that does not thrill me as it did before.

What I find beautiful in Paris are the young couples who stroll together arm in arm, and the carefree children I see in the parks.   These—only these, it seems—cheer me up a bit.

You, sir!   In the grey, well-tailored suit!   Slow down!   Why do you hurry so?   Your face is pinched and drawn and your knuckles are white around the handle of your briefcase.   It's true that here in Paris the norm is for people to rush to get anywhere.

The young people who carry those very large green folders—they are art students.

I made a brief tour of the eleventh and twentieth *arrondissements* today. Buildings, boulevards, cafés, trees, Cemetery Père Lachaise, a nice gardener. Terribly sorry, say what you like, but I am not terribly fond of Paris.

9: Falling apart
9 March

00:01 Not at all a good day. Panic, anguish. Again I cried in the street: the tears were flowing, I kept walking, sobs threatened to rise. I felt desperate. I did not want to come back to this cold, miniscule hole in the wall. What did I do? I tried to phone Suzel. I needed terribly just to talk with someone. She was not home. I told her mother I would try again later. I came home. I knocked at Jean-Claude's door, although I hardly know him. Not home. Nor Patrice.

Nothing else remained but to go into my room. Anguish, tears, complete solitude. I opened the slanting window to the night and there was nothingness all around. Then I heard someone in the hall open a door.

"Patrice?"

Not Patrice.

I went out to see who it could be: a small brunette woman I'd seen before in the hall. Very thin, skeletal. "So it wasn't Patrice, then?" I asked lamely, tears running down my face. She invited me to her room for coffee. *"J'aimerais ça, merci,"* I said.

Alice, French, has her problems, too. She has that sickness where one is exaggeratedly afraid of getting fat and so becomes much too thin. Also, she is out of work. She takes tablets to get to sleep and is not interested in men, finding herself unattractive and preferring the sort of happiness she gets with the sleeping pills.

This world is tragic! So many are alone, sad, without money, burdened with problems and complexes! Oh God, how we need help!

I talked with Alice for a long time. I told her my story, too, and why I was crying. I felt painfully alone. My room disgusted me—I felt I was suffocating to death in there. I didn't want my lodgings to spoil my time in Paris: this was too important an experience to waste. Alice understood, as she has lived in the building for seven years. She had another, smaller room before, next to mine. Now she has two rooms. There is space here, thank God, at least enough in which to circulate a bit. In my room I have the feeling that I can't stand up without being too big. As I told her, I should have listened to my intuition. It is never wrong, and I know this. She said that the Italian who lived in my room before me had the same reaction I'm having—he felt painfully alone. He stayed only a short time.

Alice: seven years on this grey floor. And most of them in a hole like mine.

I am going to fight for the poor people! It is only the rich who live well. The poor are left to struggle through unbelievable ugliness.

Alice, too, has known the tight embrace of anguish. Her girlfriends also feel the pinch of unhappiness, as they also live alone. But things are going better now, she says. I offered her some money. She refused, but I said that if ever she should be in need, she must not hesitate to ask me.

Alice says Paris is not the same as before. Before, there was a spirit of comradeship; people readily spoke to one another. Now, she says, people are cold and in a hurry. But isn't everything a function of whom you know? I feel this to be true.

I tried to give her self-confidence a boost. I said that even though she was thin, she was pretty and very nice, and that it was one's personality, the interior depths of a person, that counted, not the externals. I told her how even with my own problems I had met a man who seemed to like me a lot.

At ten-thirty I came back to my room, having thanked Alice for her kindness, for having shared her company with me. I was truly grateful. Then, here, I knew I would have to move out. I am going to move out. I went down to the street to call Suzel to ask her advice. She was home. She agrees that the best thing to do would be to find a new flat. She's even going to look around for me—she knows a load of different people, and I will see her this Friday at a party in the sixth *arrondissement*. How kind she is! What a friend! "I would thank you a thousand times," I told her, if she could find something for me. She didn't want to give me hopes too soon, but she said that already she thinks she knows of a girl who is looking for roomers in her flat. It's near the Champs Elysées at about 500F a month. That would work.

Tomorrow I shall start to look. From nine to eleven I have a study session for the Renaissance, and at seven I'm to meet Agon for dinner. Between eleven and seven I will do nothing but look for a room. I would prefer to start all over here in Paris rather than be miserable in this little hole for three whole months. It would be a crime to spoil the second half of my year in France because of my lodgings. And 500F—the average I'd pay for rent somewhere else—is not so very much more than the 300F-plus-heat that I'm paying here.

—I'm hungry all of a sudden! I ate a *flan*, an orange, and a *limonade* in a café at six to avoid the *resto-u* this evening. It's true that I'm losing weight, and I've got this cold, too—

Jean-Claude next door just returned.

00:50   I've just spoken with Jean-Claude, and now I'm not sure what to do. He is very active and so not very often in his room. But he says the heat doesn't cost much. Good to know. Maybe I'm overreacting. Maybe, quite simply, I've been spoiled by the experience in Pau lodging with Fleur. I miss having a kitchen, having space, being around people. Nevertheless, the location is good here. Jean-Claude has at least given me another point of view, a less negative one than Alice's.

I am going to look around a bit tomorrow nonetheless. I'll spend the day at it, and I'll talk it all over with Agon later. I do *not* want to do any more crying in the street, like a crazy woman. That spoils everything. What's terrible is that I can very well cry in the street without a single person who passes by giving a damn—that's the tragedy.

10: Do or die!
9 March continued
11:00   Everything seems to be collapsing at my feet. This history course is incomprehensible to me and I'm finding the professor very bad.

12:20   I feel like being courageous. The weather is lovely, after all (how much brighter life seems during the daytime as compared to during the night!), and I am a person capable of taking the punches. I did some thinking in bed last night. "I am going to fight for the poor people!" I had written, and what then had I decided to do?

Escape from this floor of poor people and find myself instead a nice, comfy, middle-class apartment! *Hypocrite!*

Thus, I feel like staying here, talking with Patrice and Alice and even others in order to get their points of view, and undergo—for the first time in my life—a living situation that is not a rose garden. Three more months. Well, during these three months I can very well summon a bit of courage and adapt, continue to live in my little pigeon hole, eat in the often poor-quality *resto-us*, and use, here on our grey floor (have I mentioned this lurid detail?), the shared *toilettes à la turque*.

Spoiled girl! You're near to the Sorbonne, near to the Luxembourg Gardens—an ideal location in the Quartier Latin. You have a place to take showers. And in addition, realize this: you have found a very nice man in the person of Agon, what good fortune! And you say your situation is painful. Please.

14:10   Right now I am in a student café in the Châtelet building, and I've just read the housing notices. There are other interesting things here, too: for instance, a course in German is being offered by a native speaker in the seventeenth *arrondissement*. As Peter, that peripatetic and cultivated American, said, if one wants to learn something, the best approach is to attack it directly, independently. Act alone when necessary: you'll strengthen your character this way!

Paris is full of things to do. *Just as Jean-Claude has a lot of activities, you, too, young lass, get yourself involved in something and you'll cease being bored and lonely! Learn to deal with solitude and independence: that is, in effect, what it's all about here. Learn to be tough. No, not tough, but* strong.

How much braver I feel during the day, knowing that in the evening I am going to see Agon.

23:45 It is sure now. No more illusions. I am not at all in love with Agon and I never will be. The balloon that escapes from a child's hand: anguish for one short minute. Then it's over. She watches her balloon fly far away from her, high in the sky, and she accepts it.

10 March
20:20 I am sitting in a café. I don't know what it is about big cities that makes them so sad. The people who never cease their walking up and down the streets: but it's night! It's time to be inside, in front of the fireplace, and, at last, in bed. The artificial lights which never cease their glare. The solitary figures who pass by, some in a hurry, others looking pensive, others looking bored. And these pinball machines never quit! *"Merde!"* says the player at regular intervals. And the music—loud and grating. And the *dragueurs* who eye me up and down and whom I squarely repulse each time by paying absolutely no attention to them. The students, so young and so thin, with hollowed-out faces: I've never seen so many thin people as here in Paris. The youths who travel in bands to the

cinemas, the bars, to I-don't-know-where—to escape for a while.

I'm feeling irritated here in this *brasserie* and find myself incapable of continuing to write. I'm going home.

21:30 Remarkable, the effect that fresh flowers can have on a room, placed in a pretty vase. I'm keeping the room. These past few days have been a crisis for me—tears, panic—but I sense that all will start to go better, from this moment. I must keep reminding myself that one always needs time to get used to a new place. I've been here for just over three weeks, that's all, and Paris is surely a shock to whomever comes here to live.

11: How to seize the day?
11 March
15:40 I'm in Sainte-Geneviève. The panic state hasn't yet left me—this was especially clear this morning, as I awoke with my heart squeezed—but now that I've got my course books, I feel more tranquil. Paris: I *would like* to like this city, and there are instances where it pleases me enormously, but these instances are nothing more than brief interruptions in the mainstream of mistrust, fear, and disgust. I hope this will change. There are too many times when I want to scream aloud, "I am sick to death of this filthy city!" This happens most often when I find myself in the midst of too many people. I begin to feel suffocated, sickened, like a prisoner.

Tell me: Am I really as gorgeous as the people in the street make me think? They stare, how they stare, these stupid men who pass by, and I feel like spitting in their faces. Some don't unnerve me too much because they look and then continue on. But others are really infuriating because they mutter things to me and would follow me if I showed the slightest reaction. I detest being treated this way!

Each time I see buds and tiny new leaves on the trees, I buck up a bit. I think that I will never in my life be so delighted to see spring arrive, and then summer, as this year.

I'm going to read Anouilh's *The Rehearsal* now. (I have added a lit course.)

12 March
0:30   No matter when, no matter where, but for me the simple life. Party this evening at the Center for Intellectual French Catholics (the title is not exact) thanks to Suzel. The big evening out, everyone in formal garb, the girls in chic, expensive dresses, a fifteen-franc cover charge, which included a little packet of Gauloises and matches. An opportunity to display one's wealth and elegance, but not so much one's Christian kindness, as everyone was cold, closed-up.

No one asked me to dance, but Suzel and I danced together nevertheless. I met only two or three people. They neither asked me questions about my life nor tried to make small talk with me. I experienced one moment of well-being when, in the middle of the large dark room equipped with a multi-faceted glass globe suspended from the ceiling from which were darting forth rays of colored light, I realized that all the songs that had been played for this mass of vibrating bodies had been either American or English. I was full of proud patriotism at this realization, I who am American and English.

An important remark, that last: more and more these days my patriotism is rising up from deep inside me. In Pau I felt very happy and well adapted to life, but here that's no longer the case, and I feel prouder and prouder of my Anglo-Saxon roots. I must say, however, that I love the French countryside: if Paris and I are not bonding, that doesn't mean that I don't like France, for I love the small towns and villages.

18:30 Lunch at Cuvier, where I met a certain Edgar from Metz in Alsace. *Satyrican* by Fellini, rue d'Acacias, with Edgar. Champs Elysées for a trip to Prisunic—eyebrow pluckers—and to a pharmacy—vitamin C and throat lozenges. Returned by subway to Boulevard Saint-Michel, where I bought *La Porte Etroite (The Narrow Door)* by Gide, pens, and paper. I feel that this city is driving me crazy. People, people, people at every turn. I'm suffocating.

13 March

Filthy, wicked, and frightful city, she nevertheless can sometimes please. I am in a little café where I've just had lunch, a *croque-monsieur* for 3F and a large *café crème* for 3F, along with my shop-bought orange, which comes to 7F total, which is affordable and pleasanter than the university restaurants. I have the time and the space now to write and to read my *Nouvel Obs*.

Remark: sometimes, finding myself in a pleasant situation where in fact I'm quite content, I feel the strongest sense of anguish: I want to *touch* the pleasure, I want to *seize* the situation, I have the sensation that the joy is fleeing from me! I feel desperate because it seems to me that I'll never manage to grasp absolutely everything that makes up the lovely thing. I react the same way with regard to people. It is a stupid attitude, for one can never plumb the depths of any single thing or person, and in my desperation to do so, I only destroy the joy which is possible. And then, finally, I realize that I have only to enjoy where I am, relax, and be content to be content.

I like this little spot, and for once I'm not seeing everything around me as sad and deplorable. Maybe it is because there are no pinball machines here.

22:00 Fellini sees the world as terribly rotting and decadent, people as corrupted and depraved. When you come out of a Fellini film, his vision of life remains foremost in your mind, and a depraved reality presents itself to your eyes, too. This evening I saw *La Dolce Vita*.

12: *"Man, who thinks, is a depraved animal"*
14 March

10:30 Sainte-Geneviève Library. I am clean. Bath this morning—Madame Rameau is wonderful. I'm also skinny. Instead of dinner last night, I went to the cinema. I wasn't hungry anyway, and today I feel all right. I am disgusted when I run across Americans in this city because they are usually overweight and smartly dressed—decadent, in short.

12:30, Châtelet café. With regard to my feelings about this city, it seems everything is improving. I no longer feel threatened or repulsed or panicked. I notice less often than before the sadness that surrounds me. The people I see now, for example, provoke in me not disgust but curiosity. But after all, this is probably only because I am clean and that I'm enjoying the chapter on humanism in *The Sixteenth Century*.

14:35 My American friend Peter just gave me a very interesting piece of news about a job going which offers six months in Martinique, all expenses paid. It begins on April 3. Peter said that if he were twenty, he would do it. I will think about it…and I'll talk with the lady whose address in Paris Peter has given me.

23:55   What a waste of time. Cafés, cafés all the time—sick of it. I saw Agon this evening, and I can state without the least doubt that in no way am I in love with him, and that even his friendship doesn't mean a lot to me. We went to Montmartre this evening. Quite a pleasant café, as they go, and nice waiter. Agon told me all about the elections, about musicians. We drank kirs, and I ate an apple tart. Later it came out that Agon does not believe in God. I found the singing of the nuns in the Sacré Coeur very, very beautiful—he didn't. For some reason this put me right off. But Agon had a funny look on his face most the evening, which I didn't understand. If he is in love with me—but truly, I doubt this—it will be a great pity.

15 March

8:15   I don't know what's wrong with me, but I feel horrible. God. This sojourn in Paris is just not working out. I have a feeling of fear deep inside of me that won't leave. I'm disappointed and a little puzzled about the Agon situation, and I'm worried about the core course. Which section should I choose: "French Culture" or "French Politics"? I have no confidence. I have absolutely no confidence these days. I'm shaking. I feel anguished. It's horrible. Why am I feeling so? God, I hate waking up anguished. When I am crossing streets, I almost want cars to hit me. I'm not being reasonable—I'm letting my academic courses drive me into the ground.

23:00   Banalities first: I had my hair cut today—it's very short now—and I am distinctly less pretty as a consequence. I did this on purpose: now I am much less harassed by the jerks in the streets. I am less pretty, but I am much more comfortable and free.

But: I am a coward. I went to the cultural group instead of to the politics group. Why? Because I didn't have the confidence in myself, nor the desire to work a lot, to go to the politics group, which would be more challenging. Yet I had thought about trying it, to see whether my intelligence was sufficiently brilliant to succeed. Egotist, I am, and too in-my-head. But now I feel like a coward.

I think I intellectualize far too much! My confidence in myself is never rock solid. I remember that for a brief period during the summer right before I entered university, my outlook was: *Everything is possible! Man is the master of himself and his destiny!* But for the past two and a half years I have felt at sea, rocked to and fro, uncertain of myself and of what to pursue in life.

I'm tired of always having to struggle. For some people, life is perhaps a pleasure (no: such people are surely few), but I know that for me, life is a constant battle. And this battle is, of course, an interior one, a battle inside my mind. It's true, take note: no one is oppressing me. I am free, have some money, am in the privileged position of being able to study at university. But I struggle nevertheless.

I had coffee with Kathy from the American group after class this evening, and we talked about a load of different things, including our feelings of struggle here in Paris. She reminded me that at the end of the Pau term, I was deemed the best student in the group, the most fluent French speaker who achieved the highest grades. That was kind of her, but whatever fleeting confidence I had then seems to have evaporated! I didn't let on to Kathy the depth of my anguish these days because—great ego again!—I was ashamed to admit how much I lacked confidence, and how alone I felt. Ashamed to appear weak.

But I am going to finish the year here. That is perhaps one courageous thing. *So, fine, go ahead and suffer, cry, but you are going to stay here, young lass, because it was you who chose this wretched program—yes, wretched, if you like—but you chose it, and it's your generous and affectionate father who is sending you the money that he is working hard to earn so that you can continue.*

"Sacrée Josie!" Fleur used to sigh.

I'll never do anything beautiful if I stay locked inside my fearful thoughts. And why do I so easily forget my favorite axiom:

L'homme, qui pense, est un animal dépravé.
(Man, who thinks, is a depraved animal.)
~ Jean-Jacques Rousseau

๖ Part 2 ๙

Acting Brave but Not Feeling It

13: Not part of the proletariat after all

17 March

13:20 Châtelet café. *Finalement!* I can say that the crisis is past. I think that I'm getting used to Paris. This morning was quite pleasant, and I found the Marais—rue de Rivoli and the rue Saint-Antoine—very beautiful. *Nota bene:* I do have a lot of course work to do but I'm on top of it. Another observation: I see the pattern, I begin to know myself. It's always the crisis with me before things at last stabilize, always that horrible anguish. But then I get over it and I feel reanimated and eager to do it all. All of this to make this point: one must never lose hope.

Also, I'm finding that it's not so very difficult to talk to people. Yesterday I took a little survey in the queue at the Centre Pompidou, asking people what first came to mind when the words *"individualisme"* and *"patrie"* were mentioned, and people responded quite willingly. I'm discovering that Paris does, after all, have a certain charm. And just now, I've come from chatting with an Englishwoman and an Egyptian. I had seen them before in the café, and I'm sure I will see them again. Terrific! There certainly are a thousand opportunities to explore here.

14:20 Sainte-Geneviève. Can you believe it? At this moment my feelings are such that I feel like staying in Paris for longer than planned. If that isn't droll! Yes, I would like to stay in Paris to get to know it well and to be able to travel in Europe. If I looked for a job here? Ah, how content and comfortable I feel with this coffee in my veins!

21:30 This new hairstyle suits me very, very well. I'm satisfied with it. I have to say, however, that it does not make me at all pretty. I now look rather like a boy. But it certainly is easy to wash and dry, and I am distinctly less harassed in the street, which makes me a lot more relaxed and gives me a feeling of greater freedom, freedom to walk around without being the victim of male idiots' weird words of flirtation.

I have just realized that, curiously, my dream has been achieved. I wrote about my dream a year ago: a single room where I could find peace, located in a city offering a lot of activities and interesting courses in philosophy, history, literature, music, and dance. Well, I've got almost just that! This Saturday I'm going to Fontainebleau, and I hope to go down to Provence at Easter. Droll, droll—just a few days ago I was desperately unhappy. Now, oriented and calmed down, I see the ravishing splendor of my situation!

19 March
0:55 Evening with Robert, our instructor for the base course on Discovering Paris, in order to prepare next week's itineraries on the life of the neighborhoods. Course business took perhaps twenty minutes, and the rest of the time we chatted about the most diverse subjects. Robert's

apartment is in—wait for it—the Tour Montparnasse! A hundred stories there seemed to be, all in cement and glass—horrible. And chaos reigned in the place, what with the television's blare, his kids' antics, and the neighbors' comings and goings. After this evening I now have a better understanding of Kafka and Fellini. There is a very fine line between reality and unreality, *n'est-ce pas?*

This sojourn in France is bizarre and exceptional—I knew that it would be. Imagine for yourself the spiritual state in which you are always, at every instant, conscious of being in the midst of a unique experience, and of being a stranger. This has been my life since September. Perhaps less acutely at certain times in Pau, but the feeling always rode under-current. Curious, isn't it, a state such as this: a marvelously strange sort of limbo.

I'm now listening to music at home. I love Haydn, and there is nothing more beautiful than this second movement of his symphony entitled *Lamentatione.*

11:30 I am very happy here in my little bird's nest as long as I know that soon I will go out to do something—have lunch, take a walk, pay a visit, meet someone. Isn't it true: solitude is bearable only when one knows that it is not permanent.

20:15 Excursion to the Château de Fontainebleau. A nice but very middle-class lady sat next to me on the coach. The group, in fact, was composed entirely of older, middle-class people, all except for a young Englishman and a youth from Boston. The *château:* unbelievably encrusted with wealth. After riding with all those bourgeois people, then gaping for several hours at the layers of opulence, then having to endure the commentary of that Bostonian, who was truly nauseating with all of his *culture,* I wanted nothing else but to return home to my little Latin Quarter and eat in my simple and unpretentious restaurant, Les Balkans. I hate wealth and intellectualism!

My little restaurant was in good form. The funny portly waiter—*"Une banane à la crème!"*—knows me now, and that makes everything more agreeable and familiar. I chatted with two North Africans at my table. One was very interested in liberal, humanist ideas. The variety of people whom you meet in Paris is truly staggering. When I left, the portly waiter waved and called across the room, *"Au revoir, Mademoiselle. A la prochaine!"* (Good-bye – until next time!)

Just for the record, here is what various Parisians are saying about my French. "You speak French amazingly well—no accent, nothing!" "Are you from the North?" "Are you from Provence?" "You have no American accent!"

23:30 Ha. And I claim to know the life of the poor student. I've just spoken with Patrice because I wanted to know which *resto-u* would be open tomorrow, and I told him that today instead of the *resto-u*, I went to eat in regular restaurants. For Patrice this is completely out of the question.

When I told him that I had spent 12F (about $2.40) for dinner, he was shocked. "You've got the means. Me, I can spend only 3F per meal."

Twelve francs is not an enormous amount. And note that it's only occasionally that I eat anywhere other than the *resto-us*. I really don't know what it is to be poor. I cut down expenses by eating in *resto-us* and by doing my laundry by hand. But if I wanted to, I could eat more elegantly and do my laundry at the laundromat. And think of this: I spent 35F for the visit this afternoon to Fontainebleau, and soon I will leave on vacation in the country. Thus, I am playacting. I am in no way a part of the "proletariat" and probably never will be. But at least I'm seeing my true situation more clearly and taking the time to see into the lives of others.

14: "The face of a nun"
20 March
9:10 I slept well last night, woke up at a reasonable hour, stayed in bed a moment thinking, considering what to do today: go to Saint-Cloud? Take a walk on the Ile Saint-Louis? Visit the Jeu de Paume? See a film? How very pleasant, on this sunny Sunday! I do my work but it is not heavy, hence I can permit myself to enjoy life.

22:15 Agon and I have fallen out! At the café earlier he asked whether he could come by my room in the next week. I felt a sudden shiver of fear (*fear and trembling,* I think), and I didn't know what to say. I looked at my drink, then up at him, and I couldn't find any words. I felt I was choking on my unease. Finally I said, "It's very small, miniscule, in fact. There's nothing to do there." He was silent then, too. *"Je t'aime beaucoup,"* he began. I interrupted, "You are a wonderful friend, but…" Miles opened up between us, in the space of a few seconds. It all fell apart. He looked so hurt! Abruptly, he said that he had to do more work before class tomorrow, and he rose. I rose, too. *"Agon, pardonne-moi…"* I began, and again could find no further words. He looked down, pausing a moment, looked up at me with a sad smile, put a ten-franc note on the table, and turned away to leave. I just stood there for a few seconds, hardly able to breathe, and then I called after him, as he'd begun walking to the door, "I'll see you Wednesday, at Châtelet, for dinner." He turned his head slightly but said nothing, and he walked out the door. I sat down for a moment, feeling weak, finished my kir, then gathered myself together and came home.

Oh God. I suppose this had to happen! What exactly *has* happened? Are we no longer friends?

21 March
14:00   The problem of Agon: increasingly, and especially after last night, I feel that nothing more is possible between us, but at the same time I don't want to drop a sure friend. It is bizarre. Ordinarily I prefer solitude rather than a tepid friendship. But in this case, I hesitate to end the thing. Maybe this is because he is quite sweet despite it all, and honest

as well. But above all, if I'm frank, it's that I don't want to feel alone. I'll go meet him for dinner Wednesday and hopefully we can talk things over.

Had lunch today with a German friend, Pieter, whom I met last week doing my itinerary for the base course. It's good to meet people of various nationalities. I learned that there is quite a strong division in Germany between the north and the south. The south is agricultural, conservative, and Catholic, and the north is more industrial, liberal, and Protestant. From a pal of his who studied at Columbia University in New York, Pieter had been given to understand that Americans were easy to get to know and quite spontaneous. And the fact that he and I met and had coffee together without a lot of formal introductions seemed to confirm his friend's observation. I hadn't known that we Americans were considered spontaneous!

Pieter works as an engineer, but he wants to pursue advanced studies so as to be able to work in Arab countries. He's in Paris looking for an engineering school. He's discovered, however, that not being eligible for a scholarship here, he will have to return to Germany for a while to work and save money.

I am going to see Pieter tomorrow around noon at the *resto-u*. I think he said that he was leaving for Germany in the afternoon. A nice guy, but not too finely-tuned. It seems that what I seek constantly in people is great sensitivity: sensitivity first with regard to other people but also towards nature, art, music.

22 March
12:50, Châtelet café. I don't know why, but I am wonderfully content in this little crack in the wall, this student café. The Mystère ice cream I just devoured was delicious. At this table is an African, a Frenchwoman, and a man whose origins I can't pin down (Spanish, I think). The clientele here? There are a lot of Africans: Tunisians, Algerians, blacks. Perhaps half the people here fall into this category, and the other half is made up of Europeans, maybe some North Americans, too. I've just chatted with the Tunisian next to me. The café is full to bursting!

14:10 Sainte-Geneviève. I've just left my lovely little café. A guy next to me really annoyed me. I began to do my survey on *"individualisme," "patrie,"* and *"culture,"* talking with two students across from me, when this guy interrupted. He thought that I was harassing people. He, you see, studies human beings but by way of *books,* not by speaking with people. He thought I was making a half-baked psychological study, and he was hostile and rude with his criticism. He also made some very pejorative remarks about Americans.

I responded to him point by point. I was not harassing people: I had asked them beforehand whether they'd like to respond, and they could have refused. He studied human behavior through books? "You're studying people? Well then, you'd better talk with them!" A psychological study: let's not exaggerate. I was doing a little survey for an American course on current French attitudes, that was all. Nothing to get all hot and bothered about!

He continued to harangue, dispute, swear, and the worst of it was that the two others listened to him with their mugs all serious.

At that moment I saw my Tunisian friend come in and head for a corner table, and as he passed I smiled to him and said hello. The rude chap, observing this interaction, remarked with disdain, "She's got the face of a nun."

I tried to continue the interview since my two subjects had been willing to respond, but it had become impossible with this maniac at my elbow. So I left.

20:30   Here I am at the Grand Théâtre, Cité Universitaire. A concert of chamber music is about to begin. I left early from a class in order to come here. This morning I left the Renaissance early also because the teaching assistant was dissertating and it was nothing but an absolutely useless digression. Studies: not going too well this term. I don't care; I'll work for myself and just see what comes.

Thinking about that awful man at the café. I mustn't let messed-up guys make me doubt myself. He certainly had personal and psychological problems concerning women and foreigners. I take his insult—"She has the face of a nun"—as, on the contrary, a compliment. In sum, researchers inevitably run into difficult situations in their quests. *Courage!*

15: *Jaded at age twenty*
23 March

18:40 Walked around la rue Saint-Martin, la rue Saint-Denis, la rue du Château d'Eau—wonderful down-to-earth *quartier*. Am now taking a moment in a little café to think. It seems to me that the needs of childhood must necessarily be modified with age. In particular I'm thinking of the need to be heard and understood. This is so important when we're young. When we have a problem we run to Mother or Father. But in growing older we find ourselves more and more isolated and independent, and we must learn to accept and bear the fact that we are only rarely going to be completely understood by another human being. One just gets used to the solitude.

19:50 Agon didn't come! I waited at Châtelet until seven-twenty, then I went up to eat. At seven-thirty-five as I left, he still wasn't there. *Salaud!* It's over, that's all. It is definitely over. I would not have thought that Agon could be so cowardly. After Sunday evening's upset I was nervous about seeing him, but I was there on time. I was going to be frank with him and tell him that I wanted now to be only friends with him. I was going to be honest and direct.

Men—I've had enough! Not worth the trouble! Too bad. I will live my life alone, independently. I won't depend on anyone!

22:45   One is so alone in life: how hard it is sometimes. I'm reading my book on the sixteenth century. I feel I am living only to sleep right now, and I now understand Lily, who said the same thing once, back at school. I look forward to losing consciousness, to forgetting everything, to escaping from this world. Eight hours of sleep per night, eight hours of escape. Only sixteen to support with eyes open and other faculties functioning. Maybe I can find a way to escape everything even when I'm awake. Surely there must be a technique.

Why didn't he come this evening? Was he so crushed that I didn't want him to come by my room? Must have been. Men! Is he really in love with me? Surely not. But still, the fact that he didn't show up surprised me a lot. He is not like that. Perhaps something prevented him from coming?

25 March
18:30   Back from the Luxembourg Gardens. Some insult me, others harass me by flirting with me. But where is the man of my dreams?

I'm now planning a trip for Easter in Brittany, possibly with a group of students, sponsored by Reid Hall. I had buying fever today: maps and guides of Brittany, the book *Paris au fil du temps,* and a fat volume about Edith Piaf.

20:55   Life is absurd and one big disappointment. I went out for a supposed theater group discussion at Châtelet, and there was no one at all there. Then, the library circulation desk was closed, and so I was unable to read *Jacques ou la soumission* by Ionesco as I'd planned. I took some notes on Ionesco from the *Colliers Encyclopedia*—yes, an English source, but I wrote my notes in French; I avoid speaking or reading English as much as possible these days.

Another hassle: Edgar from Metz came by to see me at seven. Great. I've had enough of men— let's say, rather, of boys. I told him I would meet him tomorrow at Mabillon for lunch. (It is difficult to be cruel.)

26 March
22:40   Exhausted, but a pleasant day. Got up at eight-fifteen to be ready for Monsieur Rameau, who came to fix my lamp. At ten I went out to read Ionesco and got through half of *Jacques ou la soumission,* which is brilliant! Noon: Mabillon *resto-u* and Edgar. Both the food and the company were quite mediocre. Resolved to do what I wanted to do, I did not accept Edgar's invitation to spend the day with him. He was disappointed, but that's the breaks! I told him that I detested structuring my daily hours, "which means that I end up doing a lot of things alone, but that's just my personality." We decided to meet later in the Montparnasse tube station for *"Musique dans le Métro."*

Went to Pont de Neuilly and walked a supplementary itinerary. Rich city, undoubtedly. The image remains in my mind of a slender, middle-aged woman in a pale blue cotton dress watering her bright red geraniums. Very pleasant, this sector, and I must return to spend some time in the Bois de Boulogne.

Came back to Odéon. Felt like a coffee and *flan*. Crazy number of people in that *quartier* at four-thirty. Settled into a little café, I read Gide with music and the cursed pinball machines in the background.

Babysat from five-thirty to seven-thirty. Charlotte and I in the Luxembourg: the fish go beddy-by and leaves and papers disappear in a hole in the ground. Dinner: stew, endives, bread, cheese. I managed quite well in the kitchen—glad I haven't forgotten entirely how to cook. What lightning-fast eaters! Then *hop!* in front of the television. Then Guillaume and his game, a bit of football. Charlotte likes me a lot—she's very affectionate.

Middle-class kids all the way: eat fast—TV; lots of toys. Middle-class parents: eat fast—TV; golf on the weekends; live in a large, well-furnished apartment in the center of Paris; leave the kids alone too often.

Came back to the grey gods and chatted with Alice a bit, then with Patrice, and finally I am in my cubby hole once more. I did not make my meeting with Edgar. Shame on me. Too bad. He bores me. Why waste my time? I'm not getting involved with a man until I'm sure there's some value to the idea. Men are dastardly too often!

27 March

19:45   Oh my God, how hollow I am inside, how sick at heart I feel! It's raining, the weather is filthy, and all day long low-life men bugged me in the street. I wanted to spit in their faces after a while! I attract these types because I'm blond-headed and always walking alone. I am alone, but I know that I am the cause of my solitude. But what is the solution, truly? Edgar? No. Patrice and his buddies? No. Denis? A mere child. Agon? Alas, no, the coward.

Oh for a fireplace with a blazing fire! A warm house, a family... But no! I'm going to take refuge in Gide.

I astound myself each time I realize that I am only twenty years old. I feel ancient. I feel as if I have lived an eternity already.

16: After a fall, a project takes shape

28 March

22:00   I fell today coming down the stairs in the Sorbonne. My knees are a bit sore and stiff now. But just now I spoke with a handsome fellow from Toulouse *(la ville rose)* in the subway. Nice, spontaneous!   He was taking Porte de Clignancourt.   I was taking Porte d'Orléans.   So much the better.

I attended part of a classical guitar concert at Saint-Roch. Amateurs. The acoustics were very bad as well. I left early, with a fair number of others. I chatted with an American from New York as I walked out to the street. He'd thought I was French. I think the Toulousain thought so, too.

Jacques ou la soumission read. Tomorrow, *L'avenir est dans les oeufs*, and Wednesday, both of these performed on stage at the Théâtre de la Ville.

I go through phases. At present I find myself anti-social. I flee from people. I spend my days alone except when I'm in class. I've written a lot tonight for the base course.

What weather! It was obscenely cold today. A ferocious wind was blowing, whistling and flapping at my window, and it snowed. Yes, snow, and this is the month of March!

30 March
7:30   My project for the base course: how about Solitude and Paris? A subject I know well. Yet I did spend some time with my neighbors Bernard and Jean-Claude in Jean-Claude's room last night. We talked about all sorts of things, and it was very pleasant and warming.

31 March
14:05   Sainte-Geneviève. I am constantly being bombarded by new ideas that disturb my peace of mind—what peace of mind?—and make me

incapable of continuing the work I had planned. I just talked with an Iranian couple for two hours during lunch and afterwards in a café. I may be traveling with them in a week. My head filled with this conversation, I can't do a damn thing at the moment!

Birth _____ Death

Everyone arrives at last at the same place, but we can take numerous and profitable turnings during this trajectory. Courage: we think, we think, but as discontented as we may be, do we *act?* We continue as if on a moving train whose route is impossible to change! But it *is* possible to change! I advise you to get off at the next stop, and then we'll see.

But I've got to finish my degree! I can't just take off like that! There's money to think about—food and a place to sleep aren't free, you know. There's my dad to think about. How would he like it if I just quit the Pau-Paris program on the spur of the moment?

This Frenchman across from me studies history. I asked him why. Did he want to be a professor of history? Oh, he didn't know. He continues to read. He is stuck on the train. You see? All of us do only what we're conditioned to do! And why exactly is it that at three-thirty I will arrive at my scheduled class of contemporary theater?

20:30 I am not really ever clean except twice a week, since I only avail myself of the Rameau bathtub twice in seven days. This bothers me a bit, but not too much. Cleanliness is probably over-rated.

I actually enjoyed my theater course today. I was playing the piano at the very beginning, and the prof asked me some questions about that. So I spoke a bit about my experiences with music and dance. Alas, I'd given them up.

"That's a pity," she said.

"Do you think so?" I asked. "I don't know." But I, too, thought so at that moment.

Today during an itinerary I spoke with a high-school student from the Lycée Henri IV in the fifth *arrondissement*. Fascinating! Instead of Solitude, I'm going to do my project on Secondary Education in France and the attitudes of students and teachers. I was especially interested in the boy's comment that *lycée* studies, especially during the final year, were so overloaded that the students' desire to learn was killed. This will be a good project!

1 April
13:05 Café Châtelet. Fleur is here, my dear Pau pal! I received a letter from her today, and she writes that she's moved in now with her brother Eduard in the fourteenth *arrondissement*. *Chouette!* I'm going by to see her soon.

Just a few thoughts as I digest. It is remarkable to ponder how capable human beings are of adapting to diverse circumstances. I'm eating in the *resto-us* willingly now, served seated at the table with strangers, and all is well. Châtelet's food is edible, I have to admit, which is not the case elsewhere. Today at lunch I ate roasted chicken, vegetables in white sauce, cabbage salad, bread, and coffee *flan*. I eat a lot—I always take seconds. Yet I never gain weight.

Last night I enjoyed reading all my letters. My sister Max is absolutely wonderful. She responded to my letter of a couple of weeks ago when I was feeling quite sad, trying to lift my spirits. How she made me laugh! "Somebody get me out of these roses!" she wrote when she found herself at the bottom of a page of flowered stationery. Two letters from Dad, too, in which he sympathized with my feelings of loneliness, discussing and commenting very well on each of the problems that I'd raised. I also received my official grades from my Pau studies: A, A+, A+.

Discussion in class this morning (Discovering Paris) about maternal and primary education in France. We surmised that the individualist and revolutionary spirit of the French arose largely in reaction to the crushing conformity imposed on them from the age of three in the schools. This could very well be true. What an absurd and complex hierarchy! What regimentation, what loss of freedom! That's not a school: it's a military camp!

17: High spirits in Brittany!

2 April

7:50 Note: I am on vacation! Off to Brittany, with all meals included. What a delight, especially the meals included! Am aboard the coach, and all seems very good, nice people.

9:00 We're in lower Normandy. We introduced ourselves at the beginning of the trip, and what a lot of countries represented here! The girl next to me is Swedish, and there are Brazilians, Iranians, Swiss, Germans, French, a Mexican, Indians, a Korean, a Finn, Russians, Chinese, and other North Americans.

Normandy is beautiful—except for those HLM (high-rise, low-cost housing units) over there— with its green fields and its solid and picturesque family homes. These homes are more individualized in style and more separated one from another in space, but nevertheless they remind me of houses I saw in Kent and especially in Essex, England, last Christmas.

3 April

9:00 Yesterday's report. Gourmet lunch at the Hôtel des Voyageurs at Fougères: boar *pâté,* roast beef, potatoes, salad, cheese, apple tart, coffee. Heaven to the starving student! We all got to know each other better in conversation. Met Samiha, a very sweet Egyptian girl; Monique, Canadian; Christine, American; Pauline, French.

A quick visit to Saint-Malo under a downpour, then dinner at eight. Another gourmet feast. Onion soup, mussels, pork, peas, cheese, ice cream. We're all going to get fat. I sat and talked with Anneli, Pauline, and Christine, superb women. The evening's entertainment was a night club by the sea, tacky but amusing.

11:15   I am now at the ramparts at Saint-Malo. This bay is staggering—what overwhelming beauty! The sea is slate blue, the sand beige, the cottony clouds white-grey against a crystal-blue sky, and all is drenched in sunlight. I am breathing this fresh air. I am dumbfounded! I have never beheld a scene like this before!

17:10   Dinan, a fairy-tale city. We ate in an English-style pub and then, instead of staying with the group, the American and I took off alone to explore. Fifteenth-century, Tudor-like architecture, enchanting! The countryside is also quite spectacular, and I'm in love with the yellow flowers everywhere embellishing the green fields. Reminds me of summer in the American midwest, the fuzzy yellow dandelions.

22:50   I'm enjoying myself enormously. We've arrived at Saint-Brieuc. Venezuelan roommate this time, Lucia, very nice, thirty-one years old, has made a study of words and their connotations. Lively dinner during which a group of us—Günter, German; Jean, Swiss; Jean-Pierre, Canadian; Roberto, Brazilian; and I—discussed the state of the world. We were the last to leave the dining room. Afterwards in Christine and Günter's room we sang wonderful four-part songs, which we are going to present tomorrow.

4 April
19:50   Delicious breakfast, as usual: *croissants, baguettes* and butter, *café au lait*. Then magnificent, splendid countryside. Erquy has a blue and pebbly bay, and there Christine and I went down all the way to the sea, two hardy American females! Christine is interested in geology and spotted interesting rocks: quartz, rose granite, and of course sea shells. Later, golden sands and a wide beach. The tide here is very pronounced. On to Cap Fréhel and amazing cliffs. I love the colors here, the blue, the green, the yellow, and overhead the white-grey, a splendid combination.

5 April
0:45   What a party we had this evening! We sang all the songs from all the countries, then we danced, danced, danced. I danced for them, alone and then with Roberto, the Brazilian, and the experience was fantastic. It was everything I could have wanted: the music inside of me, supercharging me, filling me with energy and passion. How I danced!

10:45 Things are going marvelously. Here we are in the countryside beside a very blue lake. I spoke with the Russians just now. I can't deny it: it is a bit peculiar to talk with a Russian, being American, and knowing that our two governments detest each other. I am seated next to Michel, Lebanese, who seems to be an excellent fellow.

23:45 Marvels on this trip such that words cannot fully describe. I am speaking with so many people about so many varied topics. This is a unique experience. I spent some time with Günter today. He is a good, straight-forward soul. I like Jean-Pierre the Canadian a lot. His accent is cute and I like his sense of humor. He explained to me the Québec situation and we examined my map. Hans is also nice, one of the Swiss. He is relaxed, funny, direct, but not in the same way as Günter. Günter is slow and conscientious. Despite the fact that he is with Christine, I think he likes me a little bit, as he often desires to talk with me and sit next to me.

We sing, we dance, we talk, we visit the countryside: I am happy!

6 April
22:30 Ah, after my hot bath and cozily tucked into my bed in my room at the Hôtel de France in Brest, I feel pure and clean, and I feel like writing. This room is wonderful: large, with two windows and a private bathroom. Samiha, the Egyptian, is my roommate this time.

The Ile de Bréhat was truly very beautiful. Postcard material. The whole trip is postcard material. There was a little child in the boat with whom I played peek-a-boo. Children are the same all over the world—adorable.

Jean-Pierre, the Canadian, is extremely nice and I like him more and more. He is scientifically minded but sensitive to art and music and people, something we discussed in the coach this afternoon. In addition, he has a terrific sense of humor, seemingly simple but very subtle. And his French-Canadian accent, which I'm hearing here for the first time, makes me smile.

18: *After jolly Brittany, back to the bird's nest*
8 April

Yesterday a guide gave us a tour of Brest. Saw the arsenal, the port. The city was destroyed by bombs in 1944. It was rebuilt with streets at right angles, a very modern city, very white, very impersonal. There is a monument in honor of the Americans, 1945.

Lunch at a *crêperie*. *Crêpes* were nearly burnt, but we enjoyed ourselves all the same. Cider, Günter, Christine.

In the afternoon we saw the parish enclosures. Arched entry, carved stone cross, church, cemetery, everything in granite. Breton music playing inside. Very, very beautiful. I resonate with this style. I bought a book on Breton legends and lots of postcards for myself, and a triskele ring to send to Max.

Dinner at the Hôtel Terminus in Lorient. Simple veal dish. Discussion with Günter and another about metabolism, since I eat a lot but don't get fat:

why not? Discussion with a Brazilian and his French wife about languages and other diverse topics. I'm friends with everyone and can talk easily with them, a wonderful feeling.

Now as for today. I got up at *four* to visit the fishing port at Lorient with a few other dawn types. Small boats, lobsters, whiting, fishermen in blue, it was *cold,* moon on the water. During this outing I realized that I am always aware of Michel, and he of me. He is very shy. I sat next to him once on the coach and we had a long discussion about a lot of things: music, Paris, places to go to borrow records. I'm wild about Georges Brassens songs, which Michel has on cassettes. I learned that he lives on the rue Gay Lussac, right next to me on le Goff!

After the port, back to bed at six, and up again at nine. Breakfast and then a walk alone in the city. Notre-Dame-de-Victoire was fantastic: lively multicolored stained glass, beautiful murals, pale cement walls, very airy, open, luminous. Friendly people and an active and pleasant city, Lorient, modern but not cold like Brest.

Had to withdraw 200F from the bank. How quickly it goes, money. Must get a job once back in Paris.

Back on the coach. Sunny day! We're on our way to Concarneau. Very pleasant breakfast, during which I chatted with a Mexican about American politics, and I also spoke with Adeline, Michel's girlfriend, who is very sweet.

I sense that all the women who have either husbands or boyfriends feel threatened, at times, by me. I like to talk with the men in the group, for they are all very interesting, but the women have nothing to fear from skinny little me—with "the face of a nun."

A good lunch, lobster. I like the Korean girl, who is studying textiles. Adeline and I sat talking with her for a while after lunch.

Then we visited the walled city of Concarneau. We were all a bit drunk from the cider at lunch and so enjoyed ourselves a lot on the ramparts. We took some photos there, and spontaneously and without him knowing it, I took a shot of Michel on the ramparts with boats in the background. Some of us took a long walk together in Concarneau, and by chance I found myself at one point alone with Michel. We were both a bit tongue-tied, yet I managed to get him to talk a bit about himself, his scientific studies, music he likes. I asked him whether I might copy the titles of the Brassens songs that he has on his cassettes. I complimented him, impressed that he managed to combine a scientific mind with a deep appreciation for music. Compliments: maybe a mistake! He does not need my seal of approval to lead his life. I'm not at all sure what he thinks of me. Monique then joined us on this little walk, which was a relief for me, as I could feel myself starting to like Michel a little too much! Back on the coach, I sat with Rabia from Morocco, and Michel went to sit with Adeline at the rear.

Quimper is an enchanting city and the cathedral is spectacular! It is immensely, impossibly tall and ornate. The stained glass features marvelous colors and forms. Inside I saw people lining up, waiting to confess their sins, which for some reason I found revolting. (Why not confess directly to God?) As I was wandering around the city admiring the charming old houses in Tudor style, Michel and Adeline suddenly came into view about ten yards in front of me. They didn't see me. I felt awkward and ducked down a side street.

The visit to Quimper was excellent but too short because our coach driver Rolland wanted to go see his parents that evening and had to go rent a car. He is Breton, from Vannes.

Dinner was at seven-thirty, with Adeline sitting across from me and Rabia next to me. We played silly games at the table, we laughed, we drank cider and wine. Michel was at the other end of the table, but of course I noticed him. Once, our eyes met and he seemed to look at me with a sort of sadness. This surprised me.

After dinner we danced again, but it wasn't like before. Note this: Michel danced! He danced rock and did it well. I told him, *"Tu danses bien!"* He was very modest, self-effacing. I was extremely tempted to take him by the hand and dance rock *with* him but am glad I did not. We all danced on and on, and almost all the countries joined in.

Günter has invited me to his birthday party on April 22 at eight at the German House, Cité Universitaire.

9 April

14:40   Les Megalithes: the restaurant, not the stones. What a copious lunch! One never eats so well as when in France. A seafood starter with lobster, crab, oysters, shrimp; mushroom *pâté* and good fresh bread; turkey; peas and carrots; Camembert and Savoie cheeses; oranges, bananas, apples, pears; Breton butter cake; coffee—*ye gads!!*

This is our last day, and we were very lively during our last meal together.

Ils ont les chapeaux ronds
Vive la Bretagne!
Ils ont les chapeaux ronds
Vivent les Bretons!

22:25 We're on the road back to Paris. People are singing very loudly at the back of the coach. I want to stop up my ears because I can't stand their songs: too gay and noisy, and I feel very sad. The trip is ending. The couples—how I envy them— are going to go home together and fall asleep in each other's arms.   Other friends will go back together to the Cité Universitaire. There are still others, like me, who will take the subway alone to return to their small rooms in town, but these are not so many. Michel is one of them: he rents a room in a lady's flat, true, but he nonetheless has Adeline. I feel—

10 April
1:10 Paris. My discussion was interrupted just as I was going to write, "I feel very alone," because all these terrific friends came down the coach aisle to cheer me up. People can be very beautiful.

Monique had wanted me to tell Michel that she wanted to borrow his Piaf tape, so I walked to the back of the coach to get it.

"You're all very gay and lively here in the back," I said to them. "You're singing up a storm."

Roic, the Iranian, responded, "Well, come and join us!"

"No," I answered. "I'm too sad—the trip is ending." Then I asked Michel for the tape for Monique and went back to my seat.

A moment later Susanna came down to talk to me. She teaches theater and used to be an actress. She sang a funny song that made me laugh. I wanted to cry, in fact, was so moved by her kindness. For the rest of the trip I chatted with various people, and despite my underlying mood, at least I no longer felt alone.

We've all dispersed now, by bus or subway, and I am back in my hovel. It is very early in the morning. I feel profoundly touched by the trip I've just taken. I met a group of absolutely wonderful people. I am sad to realize that we will never ever again be together, the same fifty people, and also sad to realize that I will never see some of them again in my life.

But listen! During the general exchange of addresses in the coach at around four, to my great surprise, Michel, whose address I had not dared to ask, came to ask me for mine! But Adeline always looks at me with such anxious eyes. I would in fact love to see Michel here in Paris, perhaps at Châtelet from time to time. But Adeline looks at me with her concerned, deep chestnut-colored eyes.

19: A sad assortment of Parisian characters and the need for courage

11 April

1:00   I'm finding Paris irritating. Went to an exposition of André Masson, surrealism, and understood nothing of it. But I visited Parvine, a girl from the trip, and we had dinner, which was pleasant. Then had a little discussion on the street with an unemployed Parisian originally from Alsace, just because I felt like talking. This made me think: I don't want to be unemployed like that, qualified for nothing. Let's finish, then, these abominable studies. Paris grieves me because I am deeply alone here and because there are so many weird types roaming the streets.

I walk by a café worker and he sings out, *"¡Yo sé por qué te quiero!"* (I know why I love you!) thinking no doubt that I don't understand.

I reply, also singing, *"¿De veras?"* (Really?) and he cracks a huge smile.

Or this, part of an extemporaneous monologue (in French) on the *trottoir* today by a ragged, sad-looking man, to no one in particular:

Everyone has their preferences. Like with animals. Me, I prefer dogs. They are the most loyal of all animals. I am scared of horses. I can't get close to them. There used to be horse-drawn carriages in Paris, a dozen years ago. Everyone used to go to look at them, up close, but me, I couldn't. How to explain it. You can't explain it.

What can I say? Paris is simply this way.

I am planning a little trip to Alsace, very simple and cheap. I don't want to stay in Paris over this break. Give me the countryside, for just six more days!

7:50   Two months, two months, may they pass quickly. It is almost insupportable here. I awake in the morning in absolute silence. I am alone at the top of the world, here with the pigeons. I get up and see the traces of rain on the window. It's grey outside. I eat my apple and banana. I hear only the wind and the murmurs of the birds. Silence. Emptiness.

12 April

Another lonely and anguished morning awakening. I got up late. If I could sleep all day and all night, I wouldn't know that I was alone. Yesterday I spent the day with Parvine. We were going to go to Alsace. Now I've decided that I don't want to go. I don't want to travel with Parvine's mother along, I don't want to spend the money, and besides that, the weather is now wretched, raining and cold.

Parvine's little room is great: space, hot water, even a small kitchen. She pays the same amount as I, 300F. And after spending some time with Alice in her flat last night, I hated my room once more, so white, so tiny. I'm not very brave. I feel lonely and I admit it.

Alice doesn't help me either. She's very negative. She says Paris has changed, that it's not gay and animated as before, that there's no soul here anymore. She is trying to fix up her flat these days but she hardly ever goes out. She takes an interest in almost nothing beyond the end of her nose. But when we get some nice weather I'm going to drag her out with me, take a walk in the park or go to a café together.

Patrice, my Ghanaian floor-mate: when I showed him my fifteen postcards from Brittany, he thought that I'd spent a lot of money. Anguish! Less than 15F is a lot? I can't bear the sadness of this world. Patrice is dead-broke. He has practically nothing to live on. But he has more than his father, who is a poor farm worker back in Africa.

Patrice makes me worried about my own money. Still, I've calculated that I don't spend more than 20F a day. Why then does it seem that my money disappears so fast? Next week I'm babysitting for Madame Rameau, and today I'm putting little signs up in the *boulangeries,* offering to tutor English.

If I didn't ever leave this room, I'd suffocate, die of hunger, of anguish, of loneliness, and no one would discover my body for a good week. All I want is to get the hell out of this city as soon as possible. Courage, God, courage.

16:00   Am waiting to see *Lost Souls* (of which I am one) at the Cinéma Odéon. Earlier I had a discussion with a Spanish Catholic gentleman, traditionalist, racist, a professor of art history and linguistics. Here are his mind-boggling views (which are not mine, let it be clear!). Form is indissoluble from content: European languages are the most well-structured and therefore European countries are the only ones that have developed true philosophies. China, India, Arabia—there is nothing in these countries' writings that resembles a true philosophical system. Paris is in a lamentable state: overrun with pernicious foreigners. Universal Renaissance men don't exist anymore. Or at least the few who do remain are Frenchmen. The level of culture in Spain and in the United States is pitiful. The Catholic mass ought to be in Latin to be valid; in the common languages, it no longer inspires anyone. Formerly, the church, precisely because of its refined doctrines, its rituals, the fact that it dealt with the world in a highly intellectualized way, inspired people, stimulated them to work mentally and spiritually in order to understand their world. The abominable state of the world presently is the fault of the Jews, he declared. All throughout history, the Jews have been rejected, punished, massacred. Because of the regularity and frequency of manifestations of hate shown against them, they, the Jews, are certainly guilty, and those who persecute them are no doubt doing the right thing, he said. Currently, in all countries, it is the Jews who have the money and the power, and they desire vengeance against this world that has caused them so much grief throughout the centuries. My fascist interlocutor approved of the Inquisition and of Hitler.

What a horror! What a poisonous brew of reactionary and racist stances! I responded that Latin was obviously no longer a spoken language and that languages are above all vehicles. What is important is the message, and the more directly and easily communicated, the better. Consequently, I believed, living languages should be used in religious services. Form and content: if the form is too rigid, it kills the content. I am not very familiar with the history of the Far East, but I would bet that true philosophies exist there. I learned in my anthropology course last year that the unique phenomenon about human language is that it is arbitrary, and hence one can express oneself equally well in all languages. Nevertheless, I suppose that each language must have its special features which influence the mentality of the people who speak it. The Jews in control of everything? Absurd! His racism was truly ugly.

On the way home I had a friendly chat with a shoemaker in the rue Arabalète, a man from the Pyrénées, my old beloved home. Yes, Paris has changed for him, too. People are in a great hurry, interacting too impersonally. Yes, he misses the Pyrénées. And so do I.

The Rameau family seem to be away, and the public showers were closed today, so this is a dirty young woman writing this page right now. As for *Lost Souls:* even Venice is not the same anymore. Everything changes, everything dies!

20:30   I am relatively clean because I've just bathed with cold water and a sponge here in my room. Hair, too. The family Rameau are still not home. I wanted to know the life of the poor student, and my wish is coming true.

20: *Fiery personality brands from the youngest ages*

13 April

10:15   Alice is arguing with her father. She is screaming in the hallway and her voice is bestial. She has gone mad.

18:00   Ah, sun, finally! This Parc Monceau is enchanting. A Spanish woman sits next to me, chatting with three men. I have gleaned that she is a nanny in some rich Parisian family's home, off for a few afternoon hours. Her speech is very rapid-fire and the sound of all the rolled Rs is starting to fatigue my ears. But I would like to go to Spain this summer: sun, friendly people, happy music!

I went to the Museum of Popular Arts and Traditions this afternoon. I learned a lot, read every bit of information and watched each film. Cows-bees-sheep-horses-wheat-bread-vines-wines-weaving. I will have to go back to complete the visit. I am looking forward to seeing the traditional regional costumes exhibit.

The more I learn about France, the more I detest Paris, the great centralizer and destroyer of regional specialties. True French culture, it seems to me, is found not in the capital but in the provinces: the beautiful architecture of Brittany and its language and legends; the Romanesque art of the Pyrénées and all the Occitan culture; I've yet to see Alsace, and there are no doubt many other regions rich in particular traditions.

But Paris: full of all that sparkles, all that is monumental and grandiose. Arc de Triomphe, Louvre, Tour Eiffel, Panthéon. But do these represent the true soul of France? I doubt it.

23:00 When I got back from Censier, Alice invited me to her room for coffee. Alice is actually very nice at heart. She talks a lot about herself, but this is because—and she said this herself—it's been quite a long time since she's had anyone to talk to, and so as a consequence all her words come out fast and furiously. As for myself, I was happy to be in the warm in a pretty flat with a nice cup of coffee.

I am convinced that most of our personality is formed at a very early age by our parents. Janov agrees. (I read part of his book, *L'amour et l'enfant*, in a bookstore the other day.) Alice has a nervous temperament because her father's constant criticisms and meticulousness made her this way. "Even our dogs are nervous," she says. Another thing: because her relationship with her father is insufficient, lacking in affection, she has the tendency to be attracted to men much older than herself, men in their late forties and fifties. She's searching for a combination father-lover. This is yet another aspect of her personality created fundamentally by a parent and the parent-child relationship.

What seems a pity to me is that it turns out to be very difficult to change once we've been strongly influenced at a very early age. It's as if a fiery brand were burned into our mind, our nature. But, in my opinion, if we are conscious of exactly what we experienced when we were young, we will be able to understand why we are the way we are now, and we will have a hope of improving. Without any awareness of the earliest sources of our personality, we may be incapable of modifying it. There will be people who won't agree with me here, but I feel sure that I'm right.

Nice afternoon. After Parc Monceau, I visited the Eglise Saint-Augustin, very beautiful, even if in the nineteenth-century "modernized Romanesque" style. And then, in a radical shift toward the domestic, I bought myself powdered milk and cereal. Tomorrow a camping-gas-burner, a bowl, a pan, a pot. I give in, finally. Must do it. If I'm going to be here another two months, I am going to make them as bearable as possible.

I find myself thinking of Michel, fool that I am, and I would so much like to have him next to me as I stroll through Paris. I hum Brassens songs as I walk, and I feel like stopping by his place to exchange my Marti tape for his of Brassens. But I lack courage.

14 April
20:10   Good news! Finally I've bought myself a camping-gas, and I've just drunk my first cup of coffee prepared here in my own little hovel! What an historic moment, *mais oui!* Ah, everything is much, much better now. Jean-Claude helped me put it together. It cost only 32F, with a gas cartridge at 6F40. What a pleasure! I'll be able to make myself omelets, hamburgers—that is, *steaks hachés!*—boiled vegetables, *café au lait!* I'll be able to invite my friends to coffee at my place. (If two of us can fit in here, that is. Slender friends only.)

I spent all day today shopping for my home supplies. I loved it. I love the feeling of having my own little home. I *need* this, in fact. Tomorrow I'll buy two cups and some salt.

I was pig-headed. I waited until now to buy myself these little things that make such a big difference. *Question de fric.* But in fact I did not spend so much. Such a stubborn and silly girl I am, so often.

At noon today at Censier *resto-u* I ran into Patrice. His ideas are so different from mine, but we have good discussions nevertheless. For Patrice, a woman can never be a simple friend. If he gets along well with her, after a certain amount of time he feels driven to get physical with her. Full stop. Talking, going to films and expositions together: this is neither enough nor even possible to sustain indefinitely. By contrast, for me it's very possible. In fact, I like to have buddies, friends, without feeling driven to sleep with them.

Similarly, he doesn't understand Alice. He despises her because he finds her sick and crazy. I explained to him that in fact she is sick, that is, troubled, and that she has no confidence in herself. She's alone, too, and needs a friend. She is a human being like the rest of us and in fact very kind, not to be despised. Once, when Alice gave Patrice a cup of coffee, he was mistrustful and threw it down the WC. I told him he was wrong. He should try to understand her.

ஐ Part 3 ௸

Digging In or Digging Out?

21: Life is so beautiful—even having to use the public showers

15 April

19:55   A resounding success! A cheese omelet (I bought the cheese and eggs on the pretty rue Saint-Jacques just north of me), an orange, and a cup of coffee served in one of my *new cups*, bought this very day! The kitchen is complete. She is now ready to create miracles in cuisine! The jet-gas is working very efficiently, very marvelously. *Ô que c'est bon!* All this and Celtic Folkweave, Los de Nadau, and Marti music as accompaniment. *La vie est si belle.*

This afternoon I went back to the Museum of Popular Arts and Traditions. Fascinating. And yet again I did not get through it all.

I picked up my mail at Reid Hall and was pleased to find three letters from Max. How I adore her. When she is feeling happy, she's like a sunny day, a clown, a butterfly. What made me sad was her third letter. She described the wrenching visit she made to the mausoleum where Mother's ashes are kept. She added that she felt very alone these days, missed both Mother and me, and had started to escape the loneliness of the house during the afternoons after school by going out and walking the cliff paths down by the ocean.

Only sixteen years old, this is pretty brutal for her. I would like to be there beside her now, take her out to interesting and amusing places. My very dear sister, my "devoted sister," as she wrote in another letter. I am going to send her the ring from Brittany tomorrow with a card showing the care of the dogs from *The Hunting Book* (1405-1410) by Gaston Phébus, the *béarnais* hero. I know that she loves animals. A month ago I sent her a card with the Dürer rabbit print, which she liked very much. She's such a good soul, writing to me three times in ten days! She knew that I also was feeling lonely.

16 April

20:30   Two days have gone by now without my having spoken to a soul. But this doesn't bother me. I am too tired to worry about it. And in addition, two months will pass quickly. Also, I bought myself some terrific music today: Brassens, Brel, Stivell. Sat for a while in the Luxembourg, always gay on a nice day, the daily spectacle. Went to the flea market at Clignancourt: thieves and bothersome types, nothing of real interest, a lot of jeans and Germans. I haven't done a blasted thing all day of any importance.

I did begin to read Jacques Prévert's *Paroles*. I like this writer a lot, whom I've just discovered on account of his recent death. Parts of his *Attempt to describe a dinner among heads in Paris, France* made me burst out laughing in the Luxembourg. Then, other parts moved me to somber reflection. I really like his spontaneous, impressionist style, his nonconformist attitude, his sympathy for the poor and lonely. He strikes a positive chord within me.

I also bought a monthly today that I find interesting, *Brittany in Paris*; *Piaf* by Simone Berteaut, a good biography that is going to take an eternity to finish; and *Le Nouvel Observateur*. I'm not at a loss for reading material! All things considered, I have absolutely everything I could desire, except for one small item: a friend, a companion.

23:00   My first guest came to see me this evening—what a pleasure! This afternoon I telephoned Rabia, the pretty Moroccan woman I met in Brittany, to invite her over. She's twenty-four and writing her thesis in economics. She arrived at eight-forty-five, I made coffee and served cookies, and we talked and listened to Brassens and Brel until ten-thirty. When she entered, I was a bit ashamed of my tiny room, but she said she had a good first impression. Nevertheless, I have some justification for complaining about the place, for witness: Rabia, who has her own room in a lady's apartment, complete with WC and a kitchen, also pays 300F a month. And her friend, who has a *chambre de bonne* with a kitchen and shower, pays 300F. Then there's me: miniscule room, no kitchen or hot water, WC *à la turque*, for 300F. Yes, I could have found something better! I shouldn't have taken the first thing I saw.

17 April

9:40   I'm running after adventure! Out of sheer necessity, I am now going to go down to the rue Mouffetard to use the *public showers*. A new low. I'll have to report back on this. Good Sunday to you.

11:50   Arrived, little valise in hand, I go into the public showers and pay 4F70 (robbery) for a twenty-minute shower. I am number eighteen in line. Seated in the murky, humid waiting room, I notice that the people who are waiting are quite varied. Naturally some humble-looking old folks, but also a lady in her thirties with her little girl; a husky, bearded student; a properly dressed shopkeeperly lady; a distinguished looking businessman—this last surprised me. The good woman who was seeing to us would cry out the numbers in a loud voice. *"Onze! Qui a le numéro onze?* Here you go, sir, *voilà."* She kept a mop going over the wet floor. Some people seemed tired. Tired of life, perhaps. Others seemed quite at ease, like the bearded student. Others seemed irritated, like the upper-class businessman (are we a little embarrassed to be obliged to use the public showers?).

I summon patience and humility, feeling hot and damp, as I read my Breton magazine. Next to me a young man suddenly asks me whether it wasn't I who was arguing about education with two other students last week in the *resto-u*. As a matter of fact, yes, it was I. This young man happened to be sitting at a neighboring table that day. I chatted

104

with him for a moment and he asked me, was I Parisian? Merciful Lord, no.

"Dix-huit!"

I found my little stall and glanced at my watch. Eleven o'clock. Twenty minutes. *Hop!* At rapid pace I took my shower. The stall was lined with decorative tiles, but the water was not hot. It was lukewarm. What a comedy. Clean, shiny, and dried, I put on clean clothes, combed my damp hair, and at eleven-twenty stepped out of my little compartment. The good dame in the white apron with her mop smiled at me and said, *"Merci, mademoiselle."*

Back out into the street. Fresh air! I felt awkward walking with a wet head and a valise in hand. I wondered whether people knew that I'd just been to the public showers. But I held my head high, for I was *clean,* and that was more than could be said about many of the human specimens I saw crawling about in the street!

22: A marriage proposal!
18 April
9:25 Ah, the morning smell of fresh orange and coffee in my room. Breakfast reading: a fascinating article about the intervention of France in Zaire. After twelve hours of sleep—there was nothing else to do, and I'd cried because of all the revolting men who had bothered me throughout the day in Belleville and in the Latin Quarter—I am

happy that it is finally Monday and that classes will resume. I would like to go on the Loire Valley excursion I see Reid Hall is sponsoring.

12:50 Paralyzed. Solitude reinforces solitude. I see myself as in a film, a dream. Do I really exist? When I am assailed by the temptation to give up completely, to explode with despair, I control myself and say, "Only two more months, two more months."

19 April
0:40 Thank God, who has saved me again. I ran into fellow Yank Kathy at the post office. We ate dinner together at Concordia, she came back here for coffee and Breton cookies, and then we went to her place to continue our talk. This timid, frail girl, so like a little mouse, has now helped me out twice. She talked about the guy she just met near Etoile, and we discussed the topic of sex. (I'll leave this portion unreported.) We talked about Parisian life, the *dragueurs* who annoy us in the street, the cafés. I took a good look around her large, pretty room and saw the beautiful cat that lives in the apartment. She showed me a splendid book on art history she'd recently bought, and then we discussed the Cubists and one of the professors of art at the Sorbonne whose inconsistencies annoy me. I told her about my fourteenth year, my Age of Rebellion, and she also shared stories from her early adolescence. She was obsessive. For example, she often imagined herself *killing people*. She finally went to a psychiatrist—good thing! I spoke of my mother's death and then of Fleur in

Pau and how much I'd changed since knowing her. We talked about so many, many things, here in my hole and there in her room in the *troisième,* rue des Filles de Calvaire. The chat was very different, very refreshing, and lifted my spirits considerably.

When I returned, I wasn't even repulsed by my opening in the wall. I saw all my provisions on the shelves, the coffee, salt, cookies, fruits, pans, and the large empty Italian wine bottle (a constant reminder of my predecessor, who was sadly defeated by this room). I looked at my lovely postcards and posters on the walls, and I said to myself, "Not bad after all."

13:15   Perhaps I have no right to complain—a student set loose in Paris, etcetera, etcetera—but I find myself desiring only to leave this place. I've noticed, however, that wherever I am this spirit of despair, disillusion, and *ennui* always invades me at about this time of year.

Long live Brassens and strong coffee. I will attack my studies this afternoon.

23:10   I had an interesting and unexpected experience this evening: I saw Agon. I had eaten a good meal at Châtelet at about seven and upon leaving ran into my Tunisian acquaintance in the rue Mouffetard. He invited me to dinner at his mosque on Sunday. His bright and sparkling eyes threw the fear of God into me, as they seemed to say that he was in love with me. I didn't give him a definite answer. I said I really didn't have the money to eat there and didn't want him to treat me since he was not rich either. In the pit of my stomach I was feeling that in the end, gifts make slaves. *No, thanks.*

I went on to Censier for my course and encountered a group of students who were just exiting a classroom. Bringing up the rear, there was Agon. We each stopped, looked at each other, and mumbled *bonsoir.* He was just about to go take an exam. We arranged to meet at eight-forty-five.

For the first thirty minutes at the café we discussed the most banal of banalities. I was a bit stunned. What callousness! Finally, we bagged the superficialities and began to talk seriously. He said that he hadn't shown up that Wednesday because he'd been ill. Shortly afterwards he'd left on vacation to the mountains of the Haute-Savoie. I said, "That one evening, you had suggested coming by my room, and when I didn't go for the idea…"

"You were rejecting me," said Agon simply.

"I was not. But my room is so small, and…I was not ready for that…"

Neither of us spoke. Then Agon repeated that if he hadn't been sick, he would have come to Châtelet the following Wednesday to see if *I* showed up, and if I did not, he would then have been sure of my feelings. But, as he said, illness prevented him. All right, more or less understood so far.   And besides, I never phoned him at the hotel.

"*Tu sais,* I do like you..." I began, intending to summon the courage to suggest that it might be best for us simply to remain good friends.

He responded quickly, and quite unexpectedly: "Now that I've gotten to know you, Josie, and realizing your personal qualities, I...I would not hesitate to marry you."

Had I heard that correctly?   Wait, repeat that, please.

Marry me.

I looked seriously into his eyes and remarked that I wasn't aware that he loved me!

If I understood him correctly, he went on to say he thought that love and a close physical relationship could come with time, but what counted were the qualities of the person and the sentimental and intellectual relationship.   And when I returned to the USA, I could think it over, correspond with him, and whenever I decided that I desired it, he would accept me as his wife.

Zounds!   I would never have expected such a revelation from him and I told him so.   I smiled a little and murmured, "You really don't show your emotions very clearly, Agon."   But then I thought silently to myself, he has no emotions towards me—he only appreciates my "qualities." The bolt of lightning—we must have that! There must be love and passion for marriage to happen! I was at a total loss. I suspected that he must love me just a little bit.

"But Agon! I don't understand at all!" I spoke very softly, for we were still in the café. "If you can truly consider marrying me, how is it that these past weeks you didn't even come by to see me?" He said he didn't want to "bother" me.

My mind is in a total muddle, wondering whether Agon is unable to express himself tenderly, whether he is really sensitive, whether his intentions are genuine, whether I am simply green and clueless about the whole subject.

But in the end I concluded that Agon was rather sweet and that in spite of all our disconnected communications, he was still a bit dear to me. We left the whole thing hanging as we parted for the night.

As I walked home, I reflected on the fact that Agon loves Hugo and Baudelaire. Maybe sensitivity to literature does not necessarily imply sensitivity in human relationships or the ability to express oneself really plainly. People have called me a great Romantic, but now I am not exactly sure what that means. Enough. *Good night!*

23: *Running in the streets with joy*
20 April

11:50 I feel fantastic today! Maybe it's the lovely sweet cup of *café au lait* with Breton butter biscuits that I've just downed. Perhaps it's the balmy weather, or that I'm going over to Rabia's this evening. Or is it that I took a shower this morning in the Rameau flat? Maybe in fact it's the letter I received today from Dad, who liked the birthday present I sent him. Also, the bloke from Los Angeles was back playing the bagpipes on the corner by the Luxembourg just now. Or could it be the after-effects of having played the piano for several minutes just now at Reid Hall after an interesting talk on the French press? It's also no doubt this party at Günter's that is coming up on Friday. In addition, I don't feel alone in my impatience with my studies, for Dad writes that my sister Max "has ten more weeks of high school and intends to hate every minute of them." Another thing: I saw my *quartier* truly for the first time today and liked it. Finally, could it also be that after that talk last night I feel flattered that someone could actually consider marrying me? Lots of elements in euphoria.

I placed my little notices offering to tutor English in four shop windows this morning. I love the life of small shops in Paris: I would like to work in a cheese shop or a bakery.

I had thought my watch was on the blink, but it seems to be working again, thank heavens. With only $136 in the bank, I do not want to have to shell out for watch repairs.

23:30 *Décidément!* Today was my day. Two lovely things happened. One is that I spent a very nice evening with Rabia, and we discussed absolutely everything. We drank coffee, ate cookies and halva, and I got to see her beautiful apartment right nearby on the rue Victor Cousin. Naturally, her room is large, wood-paneled, well-furnished in nice old pieces. It all reminded me a bit of Pau.

She's wonderful, this girl. We talked about men, and I told her the story of Agon. As for the North Africans who annoy women in the street, although she herself is Moroccan, Rabia agrees with me completely: she hates it. She was raised in classes with boys and so has had buddies among them and feels as capable and respect-worthy as a man on all fronts. And now in Paris when, as she puts it, "poorly educated" North Africans bother her, she finds it really unacceptable. She told me a story also about a black African who, after getting to know her only very, very superficially, asked her to marry him and in fact was rather insistent about it. Insensitive foolish men!

Oh how many things we talked about! She has also known that feeling of desperate loneliness where finally nothing matters anymore, nothing is interesting anymore. For her, morning brings hope—*something good might happen to me today*—and evening, disillusion and discouragement. But she has finally managed to adapt, to make some friends, to feel comfortable in Paris. It must have taken a strong character, a will to succeed—traits which Alice, for instance, doesn't seem to have.

Rabia showed me a map of Morocco and pointed out her city, Fez. To be visited!

Then, the other marvelous thing that happened is that at lunchtime I saw Michel! I was overjoyed, and I now realize that I hide my emotions very poorly! Seated at Châtelet, I was eating a second piece of brie cheese, *gourmande* that I am, when suddenly I noticed that someone was waving to me from the other end of the room: Michel! I silently responded, *"Bonjour! Ça va?"* Quickly finishing my cheese and dropping off my tray, I went over to him, with stars in my eyes. *"Salut!"* I said. We looked at each other for a moment—in fact, I don't exactly know what happened—and then I gave him a kiss on each cheek.

"Pardonne-moi," he said. "I didn't contact you because once I returned from Brittany I went to Limoges to visit some friends." No matter, no matter. Had he had a good time? Good, how nice. I told him I'd bought some Brassens and Brel tapes because I'd liked his so much. But I added that if he still wanted to, I would like to exchange other tapes, especially in order to hear the *Misa Criolla.* How happy I was to see him!

Perhaps I was too forward, but I said to him, "If you would like, you can come by to see me. I've bought a little gas burner and now I can make

113

coffee." He replied (did he hesitate just a bit?) that he would stop by. I described the route to him: "Service staircase, sixth floor, the labyrinth, courage and perseverance." He laughed. Finally I said, "Well, I'll leave you. The race is on, you know," referring to the quick eating pace in the *resto-u*. *"Bon appétit!* You're falling behind."

"It doesn't matter," he laughed. I felt full of hope and joy as I left.

Once in the street I began to run, feeling a crazy kind of ecstasy. I really saw nothing around me, only his face in my mind's eye. I heard nothing, only our conversation repeating itself in my head. I ran towards home and did not get tired. I felt a joyful and inexhaustible *élan vital* pushing me onwards. I began to sing softly as I ran. I was no longer aware of being in Paris. I was somewhere far above it all!

24: *Are the gods scheming?*
21 April
22:30   I babysat the children for Madame Rameau today from eleven-twenty until one-thirty. I brought Charlotte home from nursery school and fixed lunch for her, Delphine, and Guillaume. Frightful lunch Madame had left for me to prepare: spaghetti without sauce, canned green beans, pre-frozen fish, manufactured cheese, fruit. Madame is not inspired by the art of *la cuisine*. I did the dishes and then took Charlotte back to school. I tried to chat with the kids but they were a bit cold.

Charlotte is cute but always needs attending to. Today I showed her her father's art books. She commented only on whether this or that woman in the painting was pretty. But she does look—that's what's important.

A couple of thoughts. I would think deeply about having a child, because it certainly entails a lot of work! Secondly, I would never raise a kid in Paris or in any French school. Too tough, the city; not modern enough, the schools.

My theater course: I'm not at all inspired, but it will pass. Nice prof but too histrionic. Her gestures as she teaches are meant for the stage, not the classroom. And she is too dolled up with makeup and too arrogant. Nevertheless, I enjoy learning about literature, on the one hand simply to feel a bit cultivated, and on the other hand in order to better understand my fellow struggling creatures on this earth.

I cut Luc's class today—it's such a farce anyway— to go to lunch at Châtelet. I was hungry and also hoped I might see Michel. I satisfied my hunger but not my other desire. Tomorrow, then, at eleven-forty-five: one can only hope! Then I chatted for a moment with Rabia on the rue Soufflot and went on to phone Christine, who, earlier in the day, had come by to see me while I was out. I am going to go see her tomorrow before their party at the German House so that we can talk a bit. She also has only $100 in the bank! And she, too, is getting sick of studying. Misery loves company! Let's talk about it more tomorrow. Now down to work.

Truth to tell, I love my studies, but at the same time I do not have the *strength* to do them well, and they also scare me just a bit. *Ma chère, tu as vraiment un problème!*

23:30 "Having courage does not consist in not being afraid but, while being afraid, to carry on nonetheless and do what needs to be done." *Le Nouvel Observateur,* 18-24 April, "Life and Death of Thomas Elek, my Son," by Hélène Elek. I like this a lot.

23 April
0:50 Back from Günter's party at the German House. I saw many of my old Brittany friends, Roberto, Susanna, Samiha, Monique, Natasha, Christine, Adeline, Michel. I ate too much cheese and *pâté* and drank too much wine and fruit juice. I danced a little, even with Michel, who is quite good at rock & roll. I'd arrived a bit early to chat with Christine and to help her and Günter prepare the party food.

Now, luck was with me. It was quite strange, but here is the account. Michel and Adeline were getting ready to leave and by reflex, I glanced at my watch. It showed twelve-fifteen. Oh no! I ought to leave, too, not to miss the *métro,* which quit running soon. I said good-bye to everyone and Günter escorted me to the door. Michel and Adeline were walking just a bit ahead, Michel saw me, and he invited me to take the subway with them. Good! We chatted as we walked. I remarked that despite the beauty of the Cité Universitaire with all its green spaces, I preferred to live in town. The Cité was an artificial environment where students were the only residents, but a room in town allowed a person to mix with people of all stripes.

Adeline left us at Denfert-Rochereau to change lines. And then, once more, thinking back to the ramparts of Concarneau, I was alone with Michel. We discussed our studies. He's twenty-four and about to become an engineer. I learned that both he and Adeline were French-Lebanese, and we talked about the horrors happening in Lebanon. We agreed that it would be preferable to live in a small, provincial city rather than in Paris.

We had to exit the *métro* at Port Royal because of work being done on the line. We boarded a special bus that would descend the Boulevard Saint-Michel, but then, because the weather was so fine and mild, we decided to walk and so got off. I invited him to come to my room for coffee. He declined but said he would walk me home. As we reached my street, he pointed out the building across from mine in which Sigmund Freud had lived for a year. I showed him the massive door of my building, and he asked whether it was left open during the day. I assured him that a concierge was always on duty. He came in for a moment and saw the beautiful, wide, red-carpeted staircase. "But that's not the one I use, alas," and I showed him the door to the service staircase. I pointed out my little system on the wall to indicate *I am in / I am out*, in order to save my friends an unnecessary six-story climb.

With what seemed to me special emphasis, he repeated that he would come by to see me. He'd said this once before, but this second time, there in the dim service stairwell, he seemed quite sincere as, with a frank, happy gaze, he looked at me and said, *"Bien! Je passerai te voir."* Naturally I was pleased to hear this. *"Bien!* I'll be happy to see you." Since I sensed an unwillingness on his part to perform the friendly *bise-bise* on each cheek, I heeded my instinct, controlled my own inclination, and held out my hand to say good-bye. *Au revoir!*

I'm quite sure now that he will come by! But commentary: the lightning bolt has passed. I like him a lot, but I'm not feeling the joy and ecstasy that I was on Wednesday. I suppose that love is not a constant electrical storm, *quoi*.

Another thing! In fact, when we three left the party it was eleven-thirty, not twelve-thirty. My watch had been misbehaving again and so I made a mistake! Had I known the true time, I would not have left so early, but as it did happen that way, I was able to get to know Michel better. Chance is a strange thing. Another curious facet of it all was the subway interruption at Port Royal, which allowed us to walk together. Are the gods scheming?

25: Could this be spring fever?

23 April continued

11:15   How I loathe sitting down to work! Complete disgust. Someone, please, I implore you: explain me to myself! I like history a lot and I am anxious to learn about the *lycéens* (high school students), my independent sociology project, but at the same time I detest sitting down to work! Part student, part tourist, part humble resident. Maybe that's it—I'm fragmented. It's also that once I start projects, I am not satisfied unless they are impeccably done—which they never are—and I end up working too much but never up to snuff. Also, I'm now discovering my sentimental side, which up to now I've quite thoroughly repressed. And in my bean head I associate studies with that sad state of repression. Yes, I believe that what happens is that I am afraid as a student of falling into an overly intellectual mentality, which would make me inaccessible to people.

If only I can manage to conceive of studies as a means not of alienating me from people but of learning to understand them better, of becoming more sensitive towards them, then I think I will be able to break this barrier that exists always between me and my work.

22:30   I worked all day today, from two-thirty on. Things are going better and better. I've begun my *lycéens* project and the reading is fascinating. To begin, I'm reading Gerard Vincent's *Le people lycéen.*

I'm learning a lot—much of which is negative—but I'm enormously interested.

As I was studying, I thought back to last night's party, and the pleasant images of Michel and me dancing rock, our walk home in the mild night air, and our good-bye in the stairwell set me off on a string of daydreams. Time spent with other human beings is never wasted. And yes, good heavens, ordinary life teaches us a lot! Schools and universities are not the sole purveyors of knowledge.

I also phoned Agon just to say hello, and Rabia to arrange a trip to the movies for tomorrow night.

24 April
12:00   At last! I slept very well and did not awake feeling anguished. It rained heavily during the night, pounding down hard on my skylight, but now the sun is out. I've just put clean sheets on the bed, done my shopping, and had lunch. I'm listening to Aaron Copland and Rachmaninoff. The sky is full of grey-white clouds that are moving slowly from west to east and occasionally opening up to patches of blue, all of which makes a very pretty picture. And the air is full of church bells ringing the hour. Sunday morning. I'm happy, and that feels good, so very good.

I wish Michel would come by. But first I'll have to buy some tea because I think he prefers tea to coffee, and I want to be able to serve him what he will enjoy.

Plans: a month of travel in Europe this summer, and then another month, more or less, to travel round the USA before settling down once more with the books. In listening to *Billy the Kid* just now, my heart was invaded with a fierce pride, and I imagined that instant when I'd touch down in New York: overflowing joy and an ardent desire to see my own country—amazing to think I have my own country, after all!

25 April

0:10 Tonight with Rabia I saw *When I'm Twenty I'll Be Happy*, four films about youth. Rigid and rotten school years. The thirty-six hours of a soldier's leave during which he gets into trouble. A young man who, not having been able to buy a motorcycle, wastes all his money on useless gadgets. A young man deprived of family life who becomes a delinquent and then finds himself in the chaotic world of business, where no one wants to understand him: he ends by committing suicide. These films had a great impact on me, and what is sad is that what they depict seems to be the truth. What a society we have here. I would never raise a child in France.

It was nice to go out with a female friend. We discussed the film afterwards and then went to McDonald's on Boulevard Saint-Michel. Funny! Just like in the USA but everything in French. I had a vanilla shake. Back at Rabia's we chatted with Madame Korn, her landlady, who is Polish and quite wonderful. She loved the film *Easy Rider* and has very liberal views. The Polish language, did you know, has *seven cases!*

26 April

0:10 I had two guests today up to the nest for coffee, Rabia and Alice, and this I did despite my own little desire to study. I have the impression that I help Alice a bit by listening to her—for it is always she who talks the most—and simply by being her friend. Hence, I couldn't refuse her when she came to see me this evening at about ten-thirty. She needs someone to give her a little push to find work and to get out and see friends. Her father discourages her a lot, but she has a good friend whom she told me about, and I, too, encourage her. "I am sure that everything will go much better once you've found a job and once you start getting together regularly with friends to talk everything over." Quite simply, this woman lacks courage and confidence in herself. She complains about her health and about her tight financial situation, but she must get moving. I would like to see her *act.*

Art class from ten to eleven-thirty. Picasso. Flaws with this professor: he seems able to talk about only the personal background of the painters and the technical and stylistic facets of the works. As for the rest, the importance of the social, cultural, and political contexts, he is very, very weak. This professor has known most of the great French artists of the twentieth century personally, and I think he "cannot see the forest for the trees."

Above all, he is sentimental and not analytical or very critical—this is a pity.

In the library this afternoon, a young man sat down next to me who looked the perfect part of Romeo. Before I left, here is what I wrote, in French, folded in half, and tossed onto the papers he was reading:

I simply want to tell you that I think you are very handsome—with no ulterior motive. I don't know whether you are Italian or of Italian ancestry, but you do remind me of Italy, which I visited once, and which was also very beautiful. Study well—

I don't know whether he read it. I'd already left.

Lecture this afternoon about Chartres by an Englishman. Fascinating! I love art history!

More letters. My sister has regained good spirits, after her last melancholy letter.

Michel doesn't seem to be coming by to visit. Too bad. This is a delicate business. I don't want to break up that duo, but I would like to see Michel. Five weeks now before the end of the term. Nothing's really worth starting with only five weeks on hand. But how wonderful it would be to have a man with me from time to time, to talk with, to walk with, to share the springtime with.

7:00   There are times when I can hardly stand it. Merry songs sing in my head. I long to be traveling through magnificent countryside. I become aware of my age, which is advancing slowly but surely (twenty-one in July!). I feel a desperate desire to embrace someone. I experience a crazy longing to read everything, learn everything! And at these times an ache in my heart renders it very heavy, and I feel as if I'm going to explode!

26: The boiling point!
27 April
0:40 There are *times*... I am terribly sunburnt and it's really trying to see myself in the mirror. Even without sunburn, I am always too red. How I envy those women who have pale smooth skin that blends right in with the skin of their neck. I look at them and feel diseased and distressed. I feel like a tomato on a stick. I hold my head high nevertheless, being proud, and I continue my pointless journey.

Michel is not showing up. Shy. And not really interested in me. Full stop. Agon is not coming by. Insensitive, and also not really interested in me. The only dependable result of my relations with men is *disappointment.*

Life is sometimes almost unbearable. I don't know why. I think it may be because we're always forced to do things we don't like to do, and that dulls the spirit. The longer one stays in a traditional, academic environment, the more one's brain softens and rots. One becomes more and more passive. It's frightful! Also, too much solitude brings anguish. I saw a goodly number of people today, but without a meaningful conversation and some affection exchanged, what good is it all?

I'm exhausted. To bed.

12:01 I was disappointed to notice that two films that I'd really wanted to see have now gone elsewhere, one about Alsace and Brittany, and one about the Midi. Well, I always experience a little feeling of victory when I realize that I'm *alive,* and especially that I'm *alive inside this room.* I've just done my shopping, and it gives me satisfaction to see my shelves well stocked. Coffee, fruit, cereal, celery soup. I almost bought an extra bowl and plate—thinking I might cook one day for a friend—but I didn't, since a dinner party of any sort in this little crack in the plaster would be just too ridiculous, alas!

Bank balance down to $106. I'm keeping a very watchful eye on what I spend, and I have to be careful. Still $30 in travelers checks and some English pounds, if times get rough. I'm going to phone Fleur.

0:00 I've spoken to Fleur, and we're going to see each other tomorrow at six-forty-five. Life is never sad if you have friends. We're going to a restaurant and then, I hope, have a long talk.

But money! Not being able to resist, I went to a concert this evening at St. Thomas Aquinas Church, Gregorian Chant, very beautiful, 15F. Now only 51F in my wallet. I don't want to deprive myself of experiences here in Paris, but I don't want to wake up to $0 in the bank either.

Patrice comes by from time to time. He would like to come in for a chat, to be with someone. I always say no, usually because I'm busy studying, but also because I don't completely trust him. His ideas are often not congruent with my own: remember that he did say that he could not imagine remaining just friends with a woman he liked. I am afraid that if I let him in, he might get aggressive. In ages gone by, wasn't it considered forbidden for a man and a woman to be alone together in a closed room with no chaperone present?

28 April

This country is up the creek! *Ras le bol!* I can't take it anymore, do you hear? No more! Another strike! For the past four days it's been the trash collectors: garbage piling up in gross stinking masses everywhere in town. Today at last that's ended, thank God, but instead we've got a transportation strike! The *métro* is not running, and the buses are crammed with people and on a very irregular schedule. Messed up! This country is messed up and crazy. Constant strikes and never any results!

And Fleur? Will I be able to see her this evening, given the subway strike? What chaos reigns here in glorious France! We never have strikes like this in the USA. Good Lord, we know how to keep day-to-day life running smoothly. We talk things over when there's a problem and only rarely have a strike—very rarely. Here, there's one every friggin' week in some sector or other! I am sick of the inefficiency in this country!

And the telephone! I went down to phone Fleur and the receiver had been torn out!

Then I went to my theatre class. Two other students and no professor. Obviously no class.

Why don't I have the courage to chuck the whole thing in? I reproach myself with my cowardice! But I'll continue in order to be able to go back to LA and finish my BA next year. This is the *only* reason. Otherwise, I'd be out of here like a bat out of hell.

No really, listen. The classes: the professors are all incompetent, their lectures are meaningless, and I'm through with them. Henceforth I'm working for myself and only for myself. Maybe back in the USA I'll find profs who are capable of opening their mouths and saying something intelligible and useful, but *au diable* with these French fakes!

In order to call Fleur before six-forty-five I am going to go find a telephone: there must be one, somewhere in this accursed city, that works.

"You shouldn't blush like that," says the policeman kiddingly, as I pass by smiling. *No,* I say to myself, *it's not a blush, sir, it's my natural color, I am always like a Tuscan tomato! Just leave me alone!*

127

27: *Trying to connect*

29 April

0:20   Fleur, my dear old buddy. A chapter in life has ended for both of us. The sunny days of Pau in October, the Pyrénées enjoyed from the boulevard and from the foothills, the charming little apartment with Celtic Folkweave and Léo Ferré music playing, gentle Pau and the simple life. For both of us—over. Fleur is working as a nurse in a factory in Choisy-le-Roi. She has a forty-five-minute commute each way and works eight hours a day with an hour off for lunch. She gets home in the evening at about six, climbs five stories, and collapses. She rises again as if from the ashes and gets supper together for her brother and herself and then settles down to study medicine. She says she's lost the desire to go out and that she's no longer interested in finding a husband. She is alone most of the time, and at the beginning, just having arrived from Pau, she experienced anguish, which I understand so well. She is no longer gay and zany as before. *Sacré Paris,* it destroys people, crushes their spirit.

We went to the Procope, the oldest café in Paris and the one Voltaire and company frequented in the eighteenth century. The food was okay—I had a *steak tartare* (raw ground sirloin beef with onions, capers, egg yolk), and Fleur had chicken and *frites.* We tried to eavesdrop on conversations around us but discerned no philosophers there present. Then we took a stroll around the Latin Quarter, but it had begun to rain a bit.

Back in my humble quarters, I made us coffee and served raisin cookies. That was when I noticed that Fleur was not Fleur anymore. Twenty-seven years old and she's despaired of ever getting married, but I can tell that she still desires to find someone special. She is going to travel to England and Israel, she'll receive some sort of advanced nursing certification, and she'll see what develops. But here in Paris she's not very happy. She, too, finds herself harassed by various men in the street, and we both now admit that in spite of our love of world cultures, we're becoming a bit cranky and biased in our views of all this.

As we were talking, who but Patrice happened to come by. He entered my room without so much as a by-your-leave and had the audacity to ask me for a coffee! I did not hide my displeasure very well, he noticed it, and he got a bit angry. We all talked for a bit and then he left. Thanks to this incident, Fleur and I resumed our conversation about the problems of men in Paris with renewed vigor.

When Fleur left, I watched her descend the grey stairway: it was bizarre, such a long way down, down, down, and her voice got fainter and fainter. Good-bye my little Fleur, *à bientôt*.

23:00 This has done me good! It has reanimated my faith in humanity. This evening after leaving the library I was terribly thirsty. I went to the rue Monsieur le Prince to see whether the Arab grocery store was open, and it was. I hunted around for orange juice, and not having any luck, finally asked the clerk for help. I showed a positive reaction when he remarked that Tropicana was an American brand. We began to chat (in French) and he asked me, was I American? He, I learned, was from Tunisia, "a charming country." Called Abim, he seemed very nice and so I continued to talk with him. He invited me for a drink and I accepted. We went to a café right across the way and I ordered a grapefruit juice. We began to talk and then a fat, drunken man began to bother Abim, which didn't faze him much since he was in a good mood. But it bothered me, and I said, "I think I'm about ready to leave." Abim answered, "I'd advise it," but he smiled and said to stop by to say hello whenever I wanted. He was very kind!

My day: in the morning, the Bourbon Palace; at noon, Châtelet and still no Michel; in the afternoon, reading, class with Luc the idiot-philosopher, and then more reading. About Luc: it's a pity the way the study of philosophy can rot the brain of some people. I've never known anyone as intellectually warped as Luc. But I don't care about profs anymore. I study now by myself and for myself.

Yet how nice it would be to know someone much wiser than myself, who knew life better than I, who could teach me things, whom I could admire for his inner strength, his discipline, his intelligence.

The *lycéens* are very, very interesting, and this reading is fascinating me. I think this is because my own time at high school was very emotionally dissatisfying. Perhaps I'm interested now in these kids in order to try to experience a happiness I knew only rarely during my own high school years.

1 May *(It can't be true! The first of May already?)*
10:00   Yesterday the American group went to Chartres. Yet another grand church, *quoi*. One begins to get a bit jaded. No, in fact it was splendid, especially the stained glass. When I'm with the other Yanks, I am friendly and chat with them, but when the excursion ends, I take my own path once more and don't see any of them before the next activity or class. I want to speak only a minimum of English while in France.

Anne from the group seems to think a lot about me. She seems to retain everything I've ever said to her. (She even remembers stories of wild evenings I spent with various friends back in Los Angeles!) We have good talks, but as excursions end she also seems to want to go her own way. She is a very nervous person and tends to be too pessimistic for my tastes, quite honestly, and I think that I make her ill-at-ease for some reason. Maybe it is that I am more disciplined than she, that I spend more time writing than she (she is thinking of becoming a writer), and that, in a certain sense, I am stronger than she.

Candice: now there's a brave soul. She actually *hits* men who harass her in the street. She is a very strong and individualistic girl. Sometimes I become a little—no, *very, distinctly*—uneasy in her presence. Perhaps it's the same phenomenon at work as between Anne and me.

Once more back in Paris from Chartres, I bought my dinner and cooked it—meat and vegetables—and then, despite my cold, went for a walk along the Seine to see Notre Dame illuminated. Exhausted, I came home and went to bed at ten.

But I've left something out. After dinner I went down to phone Michel. The moment had arrived. I was going to invite him over for tea. I simply felt like seeing him. But he was not home, so I left a message with his landlady. Then I went for my walk. Being alone is so tedious at times!

A piece of news: in Dad's last letter he hinted that if I agreed to it, he would let my sister come to Europe to travel with me this summer. At first this struck me as a weight placed on my shoulders, but then I realized that it would be great to travel with Max. She's fun, we get along well, and I'm now a fairly experienced traveler. I will wait for a more explicit letter, and then I'll respond.

Back to the hole. I do like my little room, in which I am managing to cook quite well. When Max comes we can take the gas with us! Coffee and omelets in hotel rooms! It will be magnificent, a trip with my little sister who, good Lord, will be seventeen years old very soon!

28: Success for Alice

1 May continued

17:00   Something nice happened this morning. Michel and Adeline came by to see me. We showed one another our slides and I played Celtic and Occitan music for them. Michel had kindly brought along the *Misa Criolla* and a Brassens tape. We were going to have a picnic lunch of sandwiches in the Luxembourg, but instead we went to a Greek restaurant in the rue de la Harpe. I felt very happy to be with them and to eat my first Greek brochette, the kind that is displayed so marvelously, temptingly, in the restaurant windows. They were served with rice and vegetables, we ordered wine, and I, so happy to be with them, treated us to Greek pastries for dessert, baklava and kataifi. How very fondly I felt towards both Michel and Adeline!

Oh but you must know how painful it is, all the same. I find Michel to be very handsome and kind, but he's "taken" and that's clear. Truly, I do like Adeline a lot, too, so there's really nothing to do but be friends with the both of them. Their relationship was meant to be, it seems. They told me the story, and they met under rather exceptional circumstances. Michel's uncle, a monk who rarely went out, took Michel with him one day to visit Adeline's father. Her father obliged Adeline to be present, although she had not wanted to be a part of the gathering, and she and Michel met for the first time. Then, a year later, they met up in France and their relationship began. They've now been together for three years. I envy them!

I had to get back to the room after lunch because I had a date for coffee with Alice lined up. *Good afternoon, dear friends. I embrace you. See you Saturday!*

Alice. Hard to write about her. All too depressing. She is a fragile, tiny woman, discouraged by her parents, who, when they moved to Alsace, left her behind in Paris. She talked about her anorexia, the hospital, the administrative complications, the loss of her job and her social security. Total depression and renunciation of any further effort to find work. This occurred seven years ago. She's never really come out of her depression and disillusionment with life, and for seven years she's done nothing.

What a traumatic thing it must have been when her parents "abandoned" her—for I'm sure this is how she understood their move to Alsace. Then, devastating to lose her job. The two blows at once were simply too much for her, and she cracked. The road then came to a dead end for her because she does not have a very strong character. For seven years she's felt totally defeated.

Now she's beginning to get over it, thank heavens, but very slowly, with much hesitation. She is still terribly pessimistic and has no confidence in herself. She sees the shadow side of everything. She tells me how the Luxembourg is not what it used to be, that now it's only the rich who can play tennis, that the concierge will surely take the housecleaning job that she wanted. *Dear God, please help poor Alice.* She thinks only about herself, and heaven knows that I, too, know the dangers of that—sure depression through social isolation.

As much as I can, I encourage her to *act,* to forget the past and to struggle right now to succeed. It may be rough, but life is always rough and no one survives without some struggle. I know how painful it sometimes is. Alice must, above all, find a job. That will enable everything else to improve. The next time that Madame Rameau asks me to babysit the kids, I am going to ask her if Alice can do it, for she needs the money and experience more than I do.

Well, now I must direct my advice to myself because I am not at all in the mood to work. I am listening to some of the beautiful music that Michel lent me. I wonder what lovely thing Michel and Adeline did this afternoon—a film, a concert? As for me, discipline, strength: to the books!

2 May
17:50   I'm again listening to the tapes Michel lent me, new Brassens songs. Michel is not possible: he does not have enough spunk, he has no fire. I must recognize that this boy is out of the question, no matter what, because he is already with Adeline. Full stop!

18:40   Alice came by to tell me of her success! Madame Rameau is ready to let her work for her and earn a bit of money. I spoke to Madame yesterday and this morning, suggesting that Alice, a French woman on this floor, take over my job since she needed the money more than I did and also needed to get back into the habit of working. I explained Alice's situation to her, her disappointments and depression, and I emphasized that she was beginning to regain confidence, little by little. Apparently the "interview" was a good one just now, and I'm very happy about this new development.

3 May

23:00   A rich stew of a day! History course is in order, but Bertrand is a jackass. He doesn't appreciate us students at all. It's only the sound of his own voice that he loves. Rabia is wonderful and helped me to correct the wording of my survey for the *lycéens*. Then out to do errands and to eat at Châtelet. But on the way: Charles! Buddy from Fontainebleau, hello, old chap! And without the Boston snob along, how nice. Charles is terrific. I invited him along to lunch with Rabia and me and then invited them back to my attic dwelling for coffee. We had a great time talking. I adore the English. Then, at the Lycée Montaigne, a surprise to find a really kind woman who helped me to modify my survey yet further. But frustration at Reid Hall at being subjected to the retrograde attitude of Sue, who tells me not to go directly to a *lycée* to ask to do my survey, because *"ça ne se fait pas en France."*

When I received a letter from Dad with a check to buck up the bank account, which had fallen to $60, I was both relieved and a little sad, as he had enclosed only a note, not a letter. Melancholia in

Observatory Park. But Alison, another wonderful English friend whom I ran into near the library, cheered me up. And in the library, having decided not to be depressed by my disappointing professors, I sat down to work hard for myself.

After dinner I returned to Sainte-Geneviève and felt nauseated sitting across from two young lovers who couldn't keep their paws off each other. I had to move to another spot.

Reconciliation finally with Patrice, whom I ran into on the street, and then I climbed back up to my perch to work a bit more on Thomas More. I am grateful for the fact that time is not stagnant but *moving!*

29: *All my past sins: ready to explode!*
4 May

18:45 Jacques Brel stirs my soul! His anguish is so piercing. His songs are full of despair and frustration—*Les filles et les chiens, Titine, Au suivant.* He cries out, he almost seems to desire bloody revenge. It is evident to me that he has been painfully disappointed by a woman—if not by several—in the romantic realm. And when he deals with other subjects, he tends to be critical and passionately biting—*Les toros, Les bigotes.* And yet in other songs he really breaks my heart when he sings with gentler melancholy about his disappointments—*La Fanette, J'aimais.* I end up feeling a lot of sympathy for this singer, whom I see as passionate, generous, inclined to give everything to the one he loves, but who has been disappointed numerous times and who has become sad and bitter.

I am beginning a big project. It's exciting: listen. At Lycée Paul Eluard I am going to conduct a survey with the students, and the principal is going to help me to do this in class. I am going to take a sample of about two hundred kids, chosen so as to have the best cross-section possible, which is to say history and French students as well as math and science students. Next Tuesday I am going to go arrange everything with the principal, who is being extremely kind and helpful to me, and with the teachers. In the meantime, I have to make a stencil of my questionnaire and buy six hundred pieces of paper!

After conducting the survey at Paul Eluard, which, by the way, is in Saint-Denis, a charming northern suburb, I will do the same at the Lycée Montaigne. The comparison will be good because the first is a working-class school and the second is quite middle-class. A lot of work, but fascinating!

While I was up in Saint-Denis I took the time to visit the abbey. Superb, very beautiful. And the café where I had lunch wasn't bad either, and I made note of some local characters. A funny feeling: I do not enjoy spending money. I am happier denying myself things.

23:50   I went by Fleur and Pierre's this evening and was the catalyst to a very serious discussion between those two. Pierre seems to be a rather cold person, less sensitive and open than Fleur, and he does not enjoy long talks with people. Fleur is sentimental, romantic, not super-rational like Pierre, and she felt depressed and needed to talk about her problems. Her old beau in Pau doesn't want her to write to him anymore, but she is still fond of him! She's also worried about her mother, who is suffering with a few medical problems. Above all, Fleur is alone here in Paris. All of these subjects came up for an airing, and it seemed to me that despite their different personalities, she and Pierre needed to take the time to listen to each other and understand each other. I was happy to see that just then, they were communicating. We listened to some music and they asked me to stay to dinner. Fleur seemed a lot cheerier by the time I left, clearly. She'd had a chance to express herself. She'd needed to talk, that's all. Solitude is death. To be avoided!

5 May
8:15 I see a lot of people, I have a lot of friends, I go visit them, they come here, we talk a lot, I learn a lot, we help each other, I go all around the city and even to the countryside, and I now have a real clock again! I'd left it in Pau and retrieved it from Fleur last night. I've just had breakfast, and I adore *café au lait,* even if it is only powdered milk and instant coffee. I am happy to be right where I am, about to read *Le Nouvel Observateur,* and I'm looking forward to the Châteaux de la Loire trip. Life is rolling along well, and I find myself happy to be alive! *Gloria a Dios!*

19:10 I swear, I would like to write at length about this crazy world and about the impossibility of living in such a world with a spirit that loves truth. Change of mood from this morning! I am really sick of living in Paris. The American directors are like any other thick-headed bureaucrats and they really annoy me! God knows how tempting it is to abandon my studies all together. Why do I continue? Because, after all, I know that I am the one doing the work, it's my own personal effort here, and to give up would be to give up my own education. But I tell you, it is so terribly hard to keep trying when you have idiots for professors, idiots for directors, sometimes even idiots for classmates.

I am tired, very tired. I know nothing. *Rien.* My skirt is blue with orange and white flowers—some are yellow. The floor is dirty. The clock goes tick-tock. Those who study philosophy become bizarre. That's all I know.

Why is life, every day, a struggle? A real struggle! To exist, to keep from letting others crush you, to keep from going mad. The final and fundamental question: What do you do when life no longer makes sense? I am desperate.

22:20 What *is* this, an endurance contest? A punishment from God? A joke? The end? The overhead light doesn't work. Laugh if you like, you who are comfortably installed in your well-lit living room with the television, or a book, or a friend. I go down to take a shower, having switched off the light. I come right back up, little Delphine being in the bathtub, and the light no longer works! It's in the wires, for the light bulb does work, thanks to God. I'm working by the light of a little beat-up bedside lamp now: the lampshade is red, stained, and full of holes. "Monsieur Rameau will repair it this weekend," but in fact that's entirely up to chance.

No bath—no light—no life.

I feel about to explode. I'm ready to throw in the towel. It must be all my past sins, my bourgeois past falling in on me.   Poverty, solitude, unhappiness: my punishments. It's crazy—I'm crazy—I can't stand it. No one thinks of anyone else but himself in this stinking world. I can't stand it. I can't stand this any longer, this stinking room, this stinking city. I haven't a real friend in the world.   It's all too much—it's not real—it's inhuman.   Madame Rameau and her bourgeois *jemenfoutisme*—she doesn't give a damn about me up here in this putrid *chambre de bonne*, this box-box-box, this cell-all-white. The whole world can go f*** itself. I hate the world—I hate everything—I can't stand it—

30: Loire castles and friendship with Rabia
8 May
0:00   I have not exploded into a thousand pieces after all. Although life is ugly and hard, if we have friends, it is bearable. The weekend of the Loire

trip has come and gone. I saw many old buddies from the Brittany trip including Hans and Cecile, Rabia and her pal, and of course Michel and Adeline. We visited extraordinary castles: Blois, Chambord, Chaumont, Amboise, Chenonceau. Each one had its own history, adventurous royalty, natural setting, architectural style—always influenced by the Italians, of course—and its own drenching charm. The prettiest to me were Chambord and Chaumont. Rabia and I bravely walked across the stone structure above the water at Chenonceau: well done, girls!

We ate very well, as in Brittany, and Saturday we spent the night in our own little castle! Five singles to a room, couples separate. Dancing during the evening—Beatles, Latin American folk. Secret passages, walks in the countryside alone and with others, fresh air, nostalgic thoughts.

One morning Rabia and I took a walk around our little castle and found among the greenery and beautiful flowers a mysterious, ruined piano. We visited the horses in the stable and chatted with Michel and Adeline.

I apologize profusely, but in spite of everything I cannot deny my feelings, and although I like Adeline a lot, I like her companion even more, and my God, it is not easy! They like me a lot too, fine, but I'm not made of granite after all. Adeline invited me over to her place for next Saturday night, a meal together with Michel, Cecile, Hans, Christine, Günter, and me. It was nice of her to invite me, the only one without a partner. So with both pain and joy in my heart, I will go next Saturday to dear Adeline's place. I thought once today that I would prefer not to go at all rather than go and feel my heart split between suffering and joy, but I know I can't stop myself. And Michel even said that he might come by this week. But one hundred to one that he doesn't!

Anne and Candice from the American group also went on the Loire excursion. I was only rarely with them. I felt horribly jealous in the coach when Candy was chatting with Michel and Adeline. I hate jealousy because it makes me ill: I feel nausea and physical pain. In spite of everything, I do like my American buddies, and we sang a song in English for the group.

I prepared my first, and probably my last, meal for myself and a guest this evening. I invited Rabia over for a late supper at ten when we got back into town. Soup, apples, yogurt that she'd brought, Breton cookies, and herb tea. I like having friends over and being able to offer them a snack. Marvelous, fantastic friends!

9 May
10:00 Michel abandoned chemistry in Toulouse. He had the courage to end something that had no value for him. I am anguished to find myself too cowardly to abandon my own studies, which I find useless.

List of things I would like:

Grand piano
Full kitchen
Large room
Large bed
Record player

19:50   Here is what I detest above all: *tedium,*
which is represented classically here across from
me by this four-eyed French girl with her different
pens and her English grammar book, which she is
reading without ever lifting her eyes from the page
and from which she is taking neat, structured,
color-coded notes. I fall asleep just looking at her.

The weather is very beautiful now, but I prefer to
be here in the library. Why? Because if I go out to
revel all day in those fantastic white billowy clouds
floating upon a pastel-blue sky, slowly these clouds
will disappear, night will fall, and I will be very, very
sad to be alone in the dark, surrounded by the mad,
swirling Parisian crowd. I prefer *to have seen* this
magnificent sky during a shorter period of time—
I stood outside for a moment and devoured those
clouds with my eyes, as my mouth would cotton
candy.

23:30   I'm writing by the light of the room across
the way, leaning on my little slanted window, for
once again *the lights have all failed:* I dropped the
lamp—darkness. I borrowed a lamp from a
neighbor in order to finish at the sink, and now I
have no choice but to go to bed. I am living a
horrible life right now apart from certain moments

of joy while on excursions or with friends. I hate my studies, I am suffocating in this room where the light fails regularly, I am frustrated emotionally, and I detest Paris. This morning I was almost in tears.

It is now raining, the drops are sounding on my slanted window, I am depressed, homesick, lonely. I don't know how I manage to keep living from day to day.

10 May
8:30   I love Jacques Brel. His words are the exact reflection of my soul, it seems, and he moves me to tears.   Here's an observation: sadness and disillusion act as inspiration for some, and as a brake to all activity and creativity for others.

23:30   I spent all evening with Rab, and what a good time we had! I had just come back from la Défense and had lain down on my bed, exhausted, when Rabia came by. We ate together at Châtelet and then went to a café for tea. We discussed many things, we danced a little bit, we laughed a lot, and we taught each other bits of English and Arabic. We also compared the Moslem and Christian religions. We spoke of our hopes and desires. She invited me back to her room, where we continued to talk about everything.   I was on the point of leaving a couple times, but each time I stayed instead because, hell, it was pouring down, and it's not amusing to be holed up in a little attic room when it's raining like that.   Also, talking and laughing with Rab in her nice warm room was much more interesting than working on the sixteenth century.

Update: The survey at Paul Eluard is actually coming about. I ran off copies of the questionnaire, talked with a prof, had lunch with some students in the cafeteria: a great time! The principal even paid for my lunch and gave me the change!

In the afternoon, as I said, I visited the Défense area of Paris, and the Salon de Mai. Modernism has a certain charm after all, and certain paintings and sculptures were mind-boggling.

I must quote from a well-loved author, one of my favorites, as this sums it all up here: *"It was the best of times, it was the worst of times..."* (Charles Dickens, *A Tale of Two Cities*).

31: Good friends are indispensable in life
11 May
23:30   Lily is here, my best friend from Los Angeles! What a joyful surprise to find her note on my door. Having come by in the afternoon while I was out, she came by again an hour ago. "I can't believe you're here!" I cried. The Spanish friends she came with were waiting for her downstairs— and you know how far down that is here!—and so we only chatted for a couple minutes. I went down with her to meet her friends and to show them where to find the Tunisian restaurants on the rue de la Harpe, and then I came back to wait

impatiently for tomorrow morning, when she'll come back to visit me.

Lily is the friend who always understands me, who always, indefatigably, listens to me when I need to moan about something. She's also the friend whose life I've always envied, a girl with many friends and many love affairs.

We were delighted to see each other. We'll have eight months to tell each other about: how is it all going to be possible? One thing already: next year she is staying in Valencia, not returning to Los Angeles. A real shock! I envy her. I'm sad to think she won't be back at the university with me next year. Above all, I am curious!

12 May

22:00 I saw Lily for a good bit of time today. We talked warmly together in my room this morning over *croissants,* apples, and coffee. In February her father died of a late-stage cancer that had lain undetected for a long time. What a terrible shock! I had met her father several times. Lily went back to Los Angeles at that time to be with her family, but then she returned to Spain. She has a lot of good friends there, is happy with the program in Valencia, and is living a ways out from the city on a farm with her handsome Spaniard. Despite the death of her father and a certain homesickness for American culture, she wants to stay with her Spanish friends and perfect her Spanish and so she will stay for one more year and do all independent projects. I think that if I had such a circle of friends

147

here in France, I would consider staying as well. Unfortunately, such is not the case.

I told Lily about my experiences, the idyllic sojourn in Pau for the first semester, the relationship with Agon, the trip to Brittany, the loneliness mixed with joy here in Paris, Michel and my feelings of romantic frustration.

Lily really knows me, perhaps the only person in the world who knows me so well. And I know her, too. She said to me this afternoon as we were walking towards Notre Dame—spectacular walking through the streets of Paris with my dearest friend at my side!—that among everyone in the world whom she knew, including her mother, it was to me that she could express herself best. I felt very honored, and I felt the same. It is heartening to feel certain that for the rest of my life, I will have such a loyal and understanding friend.

I took Lily to a good Vietnamese restaurant where we had a wonderful lunch for only 13F each, plus wine and coffee. The waiter thought we were German. I tried to get rid of an annoying *dragueur* with language that was hardly polite, but he hung around. We had to get up and go to escape from him. How I loathe these types.

Lily told me how well I spoke French. She finds Paris completely delightful, but she is a bit naïve sometimes: I explained to her that visiting Paris was one thing, but living here entirely another!

After I said good-bye to Lily at the Saint-Michel *métro,* I was filled with homesickness. I felt utterly bereft as I watched her disappear into the Parisian crowd. I felt out of time and space as I walked back up the boulevard, the crowds surging all around me. I felt apart from that world, having spoken for a long time in English about very emotional subjects. But the sun was shining magnificently, and a man harassed me, which brought me abruptly back to the real world. I decided to buy myself a silk scarf to console myself.

Just before class, I had an unexpected encounter with a poor down-and-out on the corner of Saint-Jacques and Ecoles. I'd stopped to talk amicably with him for a moment, but in the end I refused to buy him a drink, which prompted him to shout in rage that I was *"vachement dégueulasse."* I climbed the Sorbonne stairs at full speed to get away from him, and I felt perturbed and anguished by the misery in the world and the impossibility of responding to it all. I spoke with a Brazilian classmate, and then I felt crushing boredom and *ennui* as we all listened to a badly written report on *Les bonnes.* Once more, I felt at the end of my rope, that I just wanted *out* of this life. To combat all my agitated feelings, I concentrated very hard on the student at the front of the class, and by the end, I left in control once more and in fact desirous of learning as much as possible in the weeks that remained.

At Châtelet I was very hungry, and a good conversation began spontaneously among the eight at my table. We talked about religion, and among

149

several Moslems there an argument arose. I remarked, "See what religion produces—disputes! For me religion is something *inside* each of us and doesn't consist of rituals and doctrines." They learned I was American because I told them. As usual, the reaction was one of amazement that I had no foreign accent. Even the French guy right next to me had taken me for French! He and I went later to have coffee. From Burgundy, he missed the countryside, too, and he also had difficulty making friends in Paris. He was a likeable, sensitive soul, who oh-so-typically said good-bye, adding, "Maybe I'll see you again one of these days." I felt a twinge of disappointment, but not much: with only three weeks left now, what could I expect?

A windy hard rain is now falling, and my room is well-lighted with a very warm lamp. Michel did not come by today, but let's not deceive ourselves, for he is never coming by. But I am alive! And the fight goes on! I love this little hole late at night, all said and done, the light forming decorative shadows on the walls and ceiling—with Stravinsky playing!

32: *Premature mastering of emotions?*
13 May
10:00   I feel like a nervous wreck. I have a thousand and one things to do and not enough time! But I am convinced that she who continues courageously toward her goal, who undergoes, if necessary, painful experiences in the course of it all

but who does not let herself get discouraged, will arrive at what she is seeking. In my bones I am absolutely sure of this. As we say in English, that beautiful old language, "Where there's a will, there's a way." The essential task is, therefore, *to fix for oneself a goal.* Once that is done, everything is very, very direct and simple. Yes, simple, because suffering is easy if there is a reason for it.

15 May

1:00 The wee hours, Sunday morning. Here's the very packed Saturday report. In the morning, laundry and a new acquaintance, once again made in the laundromat, Gaston, Canadian. He was Francophone and his Canadian accent was charming.

When I got back to the hole, Bonnie came by to see me, another Canadian I'd met at the laundromat. She was feeling lonely and isolated in her *au pair* situation in the country. So much loneliness—don't I know it. We went out to shop. I bought Brel and Ferrat cassettes and, as my current shoes are disintegrating, Swedish sabots. Some people here dress very chic. We submerged into Saturday-afternoon Paris, like real tourists in the crowd—and what a crowd! A crazy world of people. I hate Paris. I find the whole environment savage. Happily, as Bonnie and I were two girls together, the weirdos left us alone.

Bonnie is everything that I am not: she loves clothes, is usually very, very sociable, likes to sew, doesn't mix with the French but rather with the

Anglophones in town. She's nice but too…insufficient, not courageous, not determined.

But in any case, I spent a pleasant afternoon *à la parisienne,* along the streets and boulevards— sickening. It makes me sick. I'm sick of crowds, sick of the interminable variety of this city. Sick of the marvelous things displayed in windows, of the beautiful buildings, of the French aesthetic. Sick of the grandeur of this city.

I found a hotel for Bonnie. The proprietor thought I was French. I offered to translate for an American woman who arrived while we were there. He was surprised and exclaimed, in French, "Hey, that's wonderful—you're bilingual!" Yes, almost. Most people these days do seem to take me for French. But in three weeks I will leave, will leave, will leave…

The much-anticipated evening with Adeline and Michel was a failure. We did not communicate. We did nothing, said nothing. We spoke only banalities, and it was sad. And everyone was in couples except for me. As for Michel, I felt nothing for him, nothing—it was very odd. We did not manage to get to know one another.

When I got home at ten-thirty, I went round to visit Alice because she needs company. As usual, it was she who spoke the most, and I spoke only if I insisted upon it. An exercise in patience, in the "execution of good deeds," ha! No, Alice is nice just the same. Sometimes she tells funny stories, and she's quite sensitive. But she is too self-centered, owing to her solitude.

16 May
0:15   It has just turned to Monday, this dark night, and I am dining. A sandwich with Haute-Savoie Reblochon cheese, and leek and potato soup. The meal is a work of art. I think I am extremely gifted. It is raining terribly at the moment—I love it. My new lamp here is better than the naked bulb hanging from the ceiling, which hasn't worked for two weeks. This light is much more agreeable. A catastrophe was needed in order for me to learn to use something that has been here all along. Just like the Russian Revolution. At this moment I feel very fond of my little chink in the wall, and I am happy to be young and healthy.

Went to the Paris Fair Sunday with Bonnie and Rabia. Bonnie was so happy to come along, and I sympathized with her because I know what it is to be lonely. The fair was huge, fatiguing. Sandwiches, pastries, foreign lands, the usual crazy crowds.

Bonnie hopes that she is not pregnant—ah, adventure in romantic France! She is going to do a self-test. Bonnie is very, very nice, but if Max can come over, I would prefer to travel with her alone. After the fair, I said ta-ta and came home to study for the rest of the day.

A French girl on the floor who is preparing her *baccalauréat* came by to borrow my alarm clock. I met Monica a week ago when all my lights failed. As she and I talked, I gave her a questionnaire to fill out, the same that I am using for my *lycéens*.

I notice that it is not that the French are not friendly. They are simply shy. Once I meet them, they show themselves to be kind, helpful, friendly. But it is always I who must take the first step.

Good night.

23:55   An exceptional day! My life—I must say it—is rich, extremely rich, and I am indeed lucky.

I attended my art class in the morning, a very interesting lecture on surrealism, and then walked with Anne to Châtelet. When we arrived, lo and behold, Michel was coming out of the restaurant.

"Michel!" I cried. "It's been such a long time since I've seen you!" To my surprise, he said that he could stop by to see me this afternoon. Fine! Until four-thirty then!

I went in to eat. The world was shining. I thought of Michel and of Amsterdam, where I was thinking of going this weekend. Life was beautiful! Afterwards, I went to the library to read a book on Amsterdam. After reading it, I felt deeply that I'd just been there, and I no longer felt like actually making the trip. Curious. (Well, I *was* there in 1974 for just a few days.)

Did some shopping after class and then went home. At four-forty-five Michel arrived. We did not kiss *bise-bise* because in the context of my tiny room I suppose this simply felt too dangerous. I hoped I didn't appear too terribly nervous. We talked. I offered him a coffee, and it turned out too strong. Curiously, we talked for a long time, not just chit-chat but about important things. I told him almost everything about my life since my arrival in Paris, and what is incredible is that he seemed to be interested. My friendship with Anne. The struggles with courses, and with this room. He told me also a bit about his past: there was one year when he was particularly lonely and without money. He told me the recent history of the Middle East and of Lebanon. We carried on a true discussion, and soon it was seven-fifteen in the evening!

I mentioned that it was dinner time. Cité Universitaire? A regular restaurant? I offered to fix us a simple dinner of soup, sandwiches, and fruit. His slight hesitation did not disguise his satisfaction with the idea. Decided! We needed, however, more bread and cheese, and he astonished me by jumping up and saying that he would nip down to do the shopping. Camembert and a small *baguette,* then.

I remained a bit stunned as I set the table and started warming the soup, waiting for him to return. He came back and we feasted on tuna and Camembert, leek and potato soup, and grapefruit juice. All this and Jean Ferrat music, too!

Afterwards he helped me with the dishes. He knew that I had studying to do but had I insisted, he would have stayed longer. So at nine o'clock I said good-bye to him *à la parisienne*—three alternate kisses on the cheeks—and he descended the long staircase with his cassettes. I then spent a few minutes at my window watching the lovely clouds passing slowly by while listening to the second movement of Rachmaninoff's Piano Concerto No. 2.

No, I am not dazzled, nor excited, nor anguished, nor sad, nor anything at all. I am thinking simply of how strange life is, of how little we can foresee what is to be, and of the fact that Michel has unfortunately taken the initiative too late. For I am no longer in love with him. As the strong and disciplined girl that I am, before he appeared today I had mastered my emotions to such a high degree that the passionate feelings that I had been experiencing a week ago had already been mercilessly slain inside of me. Anguish was no more. Reason had prevailed. I had reduced passion to platonic affection.

Amazing, no? There he was in my room, seated on my bed, a sensitive, intelligent, handsome, gentle, shy young man. I listened to him, talked with him, but I didn't feel anything except friendship—fondness de-passioned.

I'm looking at the clouds, the beautiful clouds from, perhaps, a Boudin painting, and I'm thinking how wretched life is. I am realizing how Michel finally, finally came by alone—and too late. Or else look at it this way: I'd mastered my feelings too early.

In any case, although circumstances are indeed very good now, I do not find myself in love. Pity! But good friends are good, too. Long live Reason and Discipline! And let's please close this ridiculous window.

33: A whole new slice of French society
17 May

22:30   This really is too remarkable to ignore. I must describe it. The Middle Ages live on in France, but with a modern twist! The noble, chivalric spirit is not yet dead by any means. I have just spent three hours at the home of a little noblewoman whom one must see and listen to, to believe. She is Constance, from my history class, and we agreed to meet at her place to review our class notes in preparation for the final exam.

So I arrive at the rue de Javel in the fifteenth *arrondissement*. A construction project—or a demolition—is happening across the street. Constance's is a modern concrete building, quite ordinary. I take the elevator, which is a nice change from my service stairway, to the sixth floor. I'll find her door when I get there. But not at all, for the entire sixth floor is theirs!

Constance invites me to come in. A small, slender woman with dark hair and smooth, pale skin, she is wearing a sort of green wool pinafore with a red blouse underneath. She is nervous. What I mean is, it is her character to be a bit anxious and hurried. "Slow people horrify me," she said on one occasion.

I ask if I might have a tour of the apartment, for it is obviously quite large and something quite different from my little maid's room. Three bedrooms, bathroom, WC, large and attractive kitchen, a cherry-wood dining table, a study, a big living room furnished very elegantly with sofa and chairs in pale blue velvet, a large wide bookcase filled with leather-bound books, other smaller tables here and there, and on the wall three surprising items, an authentic seventeenth-century tapestry and two portraits, one of Constance's mother, one of her father. She belongs to a noble family. I am impressed with all this, and she is proud, in spite of herself, and likes observing my reactions.

Before we begin studying, she shows me photos of her two daughters, naturally. They are sweet and pretty. And they say *"vous"* to their mother (the formal form of "you").

"They say *'vous'* to you? But...why?"

Because there is nothing dearer to Constance's heart than respect. Yes, indeed, and to truly inculcate this, you must start right from the beginning. Constance even says *"vous"* to her cousins. But to return to the children. They go to a Jesuit school where all the teachers are nuns; Constance went there, too. Later I actually get to see these young girls, charming creatures, and, effectively, very well-behaved and respectful.

"Bonjour, Madame," they greet me in all seriousness and solemnity, and Constance corrects them by explaining that I am *"Mademoiselle."* "'*Madame*' for married ladies, and *'Mademoiselle'* for ladies who are not married." They interrupt our conversation a bit later, wanting to show Constance the drawings and projects they have done at school. Constance says, *"Très bien, très, très bien,"* and dismisses them as quickly. But not before saying to one of the girls, "You look disgusting! Go wash your hands. And a stroke of the comb wouldn't do any harm." The girls' dresses are pale pink and identically matching. Curious, I ask Constance where she bought them. "Oh, at a sale at Prisunic—I don't remember."

As for her husband Henri, can you doubt that he, too, is noble—pardon me, for Constance says that this term is presently meaningless. Let's say rather "of good family." She shows me a photo of him. A pure and intelligent-looking face, an air of elegance, the essence of good upbringing. She shows me a photo of the two of them on their wedding day—a handsome couple!

Constance could never have married someone beneath her social level—how horrifying, the mere thought! She can very well be acquainted with ordinary people, of course—*"Je ne suis pas snob"*— but the relationship will not go much further. (I am convinced that the only reason she consented to study with me and then later invited me to dinner was that as an American, I am something exotic.) She tells me that in choosing to marry Henri, she first made a list of his qualities. Then she studied the list carefully and decided to marry him.

Constance was as pure as the driven snow when she married. And she is proud of this. Physical beauty counts *"énormément"* for her. She is proud to be slim because her girls can say, unlike other children with fat old mothers, "My *maman* is slim." Beauty counts also for her husband, who, in front of a pimply postal clerk, was revolted and could focus only upon his papers and envelopes. "Oh it was horrible."

I imagine so. Life is full of filth, isn't it so, teeming with unpleasant sights, alas!

As for this nobleman, this gentleman whose family dates from the time of Louis XII or even further back in the glorious history of this great country which is *La France*, he is an engineer, having studied at one of the *Grandes Ecoles*. He is currently working in Brittany.

"En Bretagne?"

Yes, because although this is far away, although the children miss their father very much, it is worth it because he earns twice as much in Brittany as he would in Paris. And why, then, do they need so awfully much money? In a subtle, roundabout way, I discover the reason. Constance has problems bearing children. She needs expensive drugs in order to succeed. She indicates the smaller one.

"This one cost me a million."

A million francs? Wait, let me put that into current 1977 US dollars. $200,000? Is it possible? What is this story?

"Medical insurance covered it, then," I say.

No. Medical insurance doesn't cover things like that. They paid for it themselves! I'm not sure whether you realize what kind of money we're talking about here! And note, this is not all. Constance wants another child, a third. The doctors had told her before that she was sterile, but she managed nevertheless to have two children with the aid of certain drugs, certain extremely expensive drugs. And this is why, to produce a third child, Monsieur must work so far away in high-paying Brittany. I wonder silently to myself why they did not opt for adoption: well, no doubt it was vitally important to them to pass on the family genes!

I find all this astounding, simply astounding. But this is not all. Yes, Constance loves her children, but she is no gentle mother at the cradle *à la Berthe Morisot*—ha, far from it! She is interested in culture, in knowledge. She is doing a master's degree in history. She's already done two years of medical school and four years of movement therapy. After completing the history degree, she would like to get a degree in public administration. Her father is a doctor and her mother did a master's degree in theology. One of her sisters has a degree in French and writes secondary school textbooks, one of which Constance shows me. A lovely book, with photos, various sorts of reproductions, literary quotes. Her other sisters are also pursuing advanced studies in various subjects. The whole family is that way—they're all very *driven*. Which, Constance remarks, doesn't necessarily mean *intelligent*.

Constance does not like to cook. She has "no talent" in this area. I saw the inside of her refrigerator—empty except for a carton of milk. Since her husband is in Brittany during the week, she eats when she feels like it. Too bad for the little girls, but "they're flexible."

I offer to make omelets for them, for I'd described how I'd prepared a little meal for a friend who'd stopped by to see me and that I liked to cook. Also, the little girls had said that they liked omelets. But there is nothing in the fridge. "I must do some shopping tomorrow," says Constance.

I may return to visit them Thursday night to prepare a meal with them. Constance's husband will even be there, for it is the Ascension holiday.

In any case, she thinks that our history professor sleeps with boys. A guy from class mentioned this to her. And she says she thinks she knows my type, a Romantic, full of problems of the heart.

"Marie-Paul and I talked about you when you came into the class. We don't talk only about François I and Henri II, you know. I know your type."

Little matter if I think that the physical beauty of a man is completely accessory and that even a chubby baker can be interesting. Little matter if, as I told her in recounting the drama of Michel, I forbid myself from starting anything at all with him because of my respect for Adeline. Little matter if, for me, the sexual aspect in a relationship counts. Not as the number-one priority, but it counts. And that I would prefer to live with my future husband before marrying him, so that I would be sure of my decision on all levels. But little matter, all of that. If she knows my type, she knows my type.

This acquaintance is fascinating! A treasure trove of archaic traditions, haughty attitudes, medieval morals, state-of-the-art fertility operations, and tons of money. I am anxious to return to Constance's apartment tomorrow, to recover my notes, which I lent to her, and to meet her well-bred husband.

You don't find these sorts of people in America! Not in my neck of the woods, at least. Maybe you would on New York's Upper East Side or in Boston, but in any case nobility, properly speaking, is not really an American phenomenon—happy to say.

163

34: Strange encounters in the night
18 May

23:45   A few random remarks.   Seeing friends pleases me greatly, but I am always frightened after leaving them that I'll never see them again, for it will be up to me to contact them, and I am never sure of having the strength to do that.

I feel very relaxed and fashionable among people my own age wearing my nice new sabots.

I appreciate more and more this experience of being a student, and I am grateful for the sometimes painful situation in which I currently find myself here in Paris.

Telegram from Dad: Max can arrive in Madrid on June 21, with return flight on July 11 to New York, where we'll stay for about a week.   Need to research, but this makes me happy.

20 May

2:45!!   The wee hours. Each day my life becomes stranger and stranger and fuller and fuller of bizarre occurrences. I've just had an ice cream at Wimpy's with a French woman whom I'd just met walking down from the Port Royal *métro* station. She's into tarot cards and other devices for foretelling the future, she works at the cinema, she is divorced, and she is…*different*.

But from the beginning.

Got up at six-thirty. Arrived at Paul Eluard High School at eight. Questionnaires distributed in A and C classes. *Brava, Josie!* Owing to the magnitude of the project, I'll be dealing with just this one school, it turns out.

Lunch at eleven at Châtelet, exhausted and starving.

I arrive at two-thirty at Constance's for more notes reviewing and coffee. More strange facts: Constance uses a *whip* on the kids when they misbehave. She shows it to me: it is very old and the tip is made of silver. Her mother used it on her horses. *How can this be?*

Constance's aunt lives in the Philippines, where she owns a lot of property. She's Irish and speaks English, Spanish, French, German, and Italian— "because all the young girls learned Italian back then."

Constance adds that she has also taken a year of art history at the Louvre. "You see, you can't find a weak spot in us anywhere." She admits, however, that she really didn't enjoy art history that much. She also studied music for six years "to learn to distinguish the violas from the violins, but especially to learn the brass instruments."

The little girls in the next room are making some noise. Constance gets up and goes to them. "You girls! You're horrid *(vilaines)*!" Her voice is like glass breaking on the pavement.

The coffee she has prepared for us is, nevertheless, very good. "It's no cat's pee!" she says proudly.

I'll leave Constance now, to whose fascinating home I'll return tomorrow for lunch with her and her brood.

On the way home, I chatted with my Tunisian grocer on the rue Monsieur le Prince. It seemed that he was the only sane person with whom I'd spoken all day. When I got home I felt really tired and so napped for an hour and a half.

From seven until nine p.m. at Sainte-Geneviève I worked at deciphering *Budé, the Obscure,* an erudite thesis about which the illustrious Delaruelle admits confusion also. At nine-thirty I met Alison, an English friend whom I first met at Châtelet, and we had a splendid evening. We went to Privas Restaurant in the Latin Quarter and ate Algerian-style brochettes and couscous. We enjoyed speaking English. Privas was full of life and good food and we had a good feast.

Then we took off to see the Eiffel Tower illuminated and the fountain and all that grandeur. Alison and I discussed religion and perseverance in one's life. Her boyfriend is apparently a bit selfish: I told her not to let him walk all over her! I can't relate it all, but my principle piece of advice was to continue toward her own goals courageously, in spite of all obstacles: to be determined. Power is found inside oneself. Everything comes from inside ourselves—strength, courage, faith. What is worth the pain involves exactly that—pain, and it's necessary to struggle in life yet never despair. God will help her if she asks him sincerely and if she continues honestly, patiently, and courageously. It was then time to say good-bye, for the time was eleven-thirty.

Lately there's been no train service between Port Royal and Luxembourg, so I assumed nothing had changed and got off at Port Royal. Only one other person, a woman, also exited the train at this stop. But service had been restored so we'd both made the same mistake. She suggested walking together down Saint-Michel, and what else could I do but agree? I noticed right away that she was a bit strange, but I didn't care. She seemed Italian, as she herself observed, a small, pretty, heavily made-up brunette. Her eyes had a slightly bothersome intensity. We talked of nothing in particular. She told me I spoke French very, very well. She asked me questions about America. I told her I had wanted to go with my friend for ice cream but because the *métro* shut down at a certain hour, we could not. So she invited me to ice cream at Wimpy's.

She seemed in need of company, of someone to talk to, although later she would say to me that she had seen that I was in the mood to talk. She could see, too, that I was interested in tarot cards (hokum!) because people of my sign were that way.

She was Pisces. She worked at the cinema and lived on the rue Soufflot in a hotel. Her blue-green eyes fixed upon me with such burning intensity that I thought at first that she was mildly insane.

She told me everything I needed to know to be beautiful, happy, and well cultivated. She made out a long list of books to read, none by known authors, and things to drink. I ought to fix my hair more attractively, she said, wear a bit of make-up, and take care of my skin according to a dermatologist's instructions. Yes, she knew exactly what needed to be done. Above all, she recommended that I see a woman—at only 50F a visit—who read the lines of your palm and the grinds of your Turkish coffee. *She* could tell me a thing or two.

"That I am going to die tomorrow?"

"Why do you say that? In any case, she would not tell you that."

She herself went often to this woman, and note, these sorts of seers usually cost 100 to 150F a visit! Fifty francs was truly a good deal.

As she imparted all this information to me, we devoured our delicious ice creams. I got to see the people of the small hours there in Wimpy's. A pale hollow type next to me kept giving us pale hollow looks. Several skinny blacks, poor blokes. Typical café music was playing loudly, disco-English-American-French-pop-rock-shit. I pretended to be interested in everything she was telling me, this good, demonic woman, and she went on and on, she expressed herself freely, she told me about Versailles, Hitler, Pearl Buck, Simenon.

I learned in passing her first name, Ghislaine. She never asked me mine.

Finally we parted, well into the wee hours, after our ice creams, our little *tête-à-tête* concluded, a spontaneous experience never to be repeated. It is now three-forty-five in the morning, and I don't know how I am going to be in shape to go to Constance's at ten-thirty.

35: Upsetting omelets

20 May continued

23:59 I spent the whole day today with Constance, from ten-thirty a.m. until six p.m. It was very pleasant and very profitable on all levels. I think I will never forget the sight of Henri, her husband, as I was leaving. He had come down to mail a letter. This man who in the marriage photo was young, handsome, and strong, now is thin and seems aged and exhausted. I watched him crossing the street, and he limped a little, this skeletal figure.

Backtrack to the beginning. Rising at nine-thirty after my very short night's sleep, I felt tired and was not at all hungry. I went down to buy cheese, tomatoes, and lettuce. Then I went to catch the subway at Odéon, and I arrived at Constance's at ten-thirty. She introduced me to Henri, and he seemed very nice, which he is, and from the Midi, yet! Near to Toulouse.

I must say this. These days it seems to me that each time I converse with friends, I end up expressing my personal philosophy and helping them. Today we discussed many subjects, especially Henri and I, and truly, by the end of my visit, he was asking me questions as if I were some kind of psychologist or oracle. There were times during this visit, I also must say, that I wanted to cry because I found this family so sad.

But—to tell the story.

Monsieur believes that heredity, rather than environment, is the most significant element in forming the personality and intelligence of a child. And by extension, he said, this accounts for the superiority of the white race. I was quite appalled. No, false! I responded. I believed that the most important factor by far in the formation of a child, of a human being, was the environment. "Inborn genius" probably does play some part, but let's talk about what counts: actual opportunities and the *will*. It all lies there.

Remark: Every question, every commentary that anyone makes has in it a part of that person, his past, present, or future situation. There is no such thing as disinterestedness.

We three talked about the subject of marriage. I admitted that before marrying someone, I would certainly want to live with him for a couple of years. Eyebrows raised! Why? Because I would be afraid of making a mistake. For me, a bad marriage would be a catastrophe of the first magnitude. My friends asked, after living with someone for two years or more, wouldn't splitting up cause a big psychological shock? Of course! But so would a divorce, and divorce would cause even more hassle and headache because of the administrative elements. My view was that separation was infinitely preferable, even if children had come into the picture, if the two really did not get along well. People should never, ever use the common but, in my opinion, terribly mistaken excuse of "staying together for the children." Children can easily feel misery and loathing between their parents. A peaceful one-parent home would be infinitely preferable to a hostile, two-parent home.

We moved on to politics. Henri is politically to the right and doesn't understand the communists because, according to him, they don't realize the necessity of order and a certain hierarchy in life. He doubts that the workers can run their businesses better than their bosses. A certain training is necessary for management, after all. But I wondered, wouldn't senior, very experienced workers be the most capable managers?

Henri and Constance stay in their apartment every weekend. With the Bois de Boulogne nearby and all of Paris to be enjoyed, I found this rather sad, but I concluded that Henri needed the rest. The two of them never go out for an evening alone, they said. "Who would take care of the children?"

For lunch I prepared cheese omelets, excellent ones, if I may say so, made with herbs and very good Parmesan cheese that I had bought at my little cheese shop on the rue Saint-Jacques. The little girls were excited, for it was rare that they ate at the big table. Usually they ate at the tiny table in the kitchen. Constance and Henri liked the omelets a lot, but the girls did not. In fact, it was frightening, perturbing. The smaller one, Marie Christine, in tasting her omelet made a face and then burst into tears. That really threw me for a moment. Constance took her to her room to put her to bed.

Later I learned that she gave the girls special food because she was concerned about their health: cereal, baby food, unseasoned cuts of tender meat. Constance said that she didn't give a hoot if she's making the inevitable adaptation to French food more difficult for the children—my question— because for the present, their health was primary. So my herb-filled omelet was too strong for their poor little taste buds.

After lunch Constance had to go to a short doctor's appointment before we resumed studying, so Henri and I continued to talk. Constance had told me, by the way, that her husband was very shy, but I found him quite talkative. And he has a bit of a Midi accent, very pleasant to hear! The subject arose of arguments between husband and wife.

Henri wondered whether these were normal. Well, I said, wouldn't it be boring always to agree? I supposed it depended on whether serious differences in outlook were cropping up. Sometimes, Henri said, he comes home *"extrêmement fatigué"* and Constance wants to talk about history or some other intellectual topic. At such times they tended to fight. What did I think? I thought that this was not serious.

Now about Constance's studies, Henri told me that it was he who pushed her to study history: he disagrees with women staying at home all day with only the children, cooking, and housework. But he revealed that Constance had not been too thrilled by the idea of the history degree.

Constance told me later, when we two were alone, that she loathed disputes and that she always expressed herself in agreement with her husband, even when she did not agree, in order to keep the peace. "We never fight," she said.

Never?

No, no. She detests bad scenes.

But here is a point Constance and I agree on. We both find all the divisiveness between Lutherans, Calvinists, Anabaptists, and Catholics absurd. "How men love to complicate life!"

The visit was at an end, and Constance was sad to see me go. She looked as if she might burst into tears, as she told me she did every day as a six-year-old when she was sent to England to learn English. But she did not cry today probably because she loathes scenes. But I see that one day in the future, she may burst, as I sense that she is repressing quite a bit of frustration and sadness.

All their questions during our conversation seemed to be asking for my *(my!)* help. I felt sorry for them, this skeletal man who looks too old for his age; this thin, nervous woman obsessed by—or might we say forced to place herself in—the life of high intellect. And their young children, protected from the world in their Jesuit school, who stay inside on the weekends and are fed a special bland diet.

I came back home on foot, wanting, despite my fatigue, to air my head and see Paris. Enchanting, for it was the Ascension and the streets were deserted and the weather very mild. The rue de Grenelle was very beautiful, the decorative old facades illuminated by fiery slanting crepuscule sunlight.

ജ Part 4 beta
The Price of Confidence

36: *Reflections on chance and determinism*
21 May

00:05   This past evening I invited Monica, the girl across the hall, over to coffee, and here's yet another original and fascinating story. Monica left home at age sixteen. Later, she was required to live for three months in a home for delinquent women on the Boulevard de Sébastopol. The atmosphere there was very painful—apathy, restlessness, violence—and only rarely did she have the chance to go out. Finally, a home and a high school were found for her, but these also proved repressive. The last home was near République and this one more liberal. Nevertheless, she felt nothing in common with the other girls, and there was too much noise to be able to study well. Hence, she finally got permission from the director and the judge to live independently.

She has worked quite constantly—babysitter, maid—ever since leaving her parents, and she tends to live here and there, with friends. She is living in a *chambre de bonne* on our floor right now in order to prepare her *baccalauréat*. Given her rough life to date, she'll be very happy if she passes her *bac*, for then she'll be able to pursue more advanced studies and "make something of [her]self." She says, along with everyone else, that one can do nothing with only a *bac*.

Monica was born in Paris, but her parents are from Algeria. I did not learn what the family circumstances were that forced her to run away. She has a little brother, and an older sister who loves to read.

She told me a story about the extreme rightwing students from the Assas campus, who are apparently quite dangerous! She described how a friend of hers who had just bought a leftist newspaper, *Rouge*, was promptly followed by three of these guys. He began to run—they, too. He was saved by good fortune when a car stopped to pick him up. Another incident occurred last year at Censier when these people launched an attack with sticks and Molotov cocktails. They terrorized the students, and Monica and her pals, who happened to be there, had to flee, shaking with fear during the experience.

She said that these extreme rightists scout out and surround their chosen site—usually a university campus—with their cars and then stage their attacks to last about five minutes. This is no joking matter, clearly. One must not flash around a copy of *L'Humanité* in certain *resto-u* cafés.

In talking about the *bac*, she says that one can fail quite simply if the prof is in a bad mood. The grading is very arbitrary. The hours of test-taking are very strenuous. For example, you might have four hours of economics in the morning, then three of math in the afternoon, with geography and English the very next day.

I had her fill out a *lycéens* questionnaire. Her responses seem to be quite similar to those I've read so far from Paul Eluard. I am going to record a tape of spoken English for her to help her study for her English exam.

A very important thing about Constance that I forgot to mention yesterday: whereas for me history is a tool helping me to understand the world better, for Constance, who spent three hours of ecstasy writing her Roman history midterm, it is, she says, "an intellectual drug." A way of escape, evasion from the world. This seems to prove, first of all, that her personal life lacks something, and secondly, that her upbringing was quite cut off from real life on the streets. She is what you might call a "pure intellectual," a rare breed!

23:30   I studied at Censier today, reading more about Guillaume Budé, royalist, monarchist, elitist if ever there was one, who would like to see the people reduced to passive submission—just like the French educational system, which separates the technical schools from the academic schools in order to prevent the future workers from becoming intellectually aware of their subjected position.

And there, at Censier, I espied Agon. He was some distance away and just leaving but he seemed to glance my way. Did he see me? If so, he did not show it, and we made no contact. My heart suddenly felt very heavy but I felt rooted to the spot, and the moment passed.

I spent all evening writing, except when my dear friend Rabia stopped by to see me. For the first time, she has been with a man. She feels ashamed now, for she is Moslem, and what's more, the man is French and Christian. I told her my view: the human being has four principle needs, spiritual, intellectual, emotional, and physical, and the physical need is not to be denied. And Rabia and her *amant* are in love—so it's wonderful! There is no reason for shame.

Although Rabia loves this man a lot, she is deeply distressed because, firstly, according to her religion one should not have intimate relations with someone before marriage; and secondly, a Moslem should not get involved with a non-Moslem. Always this blasted problem of religion! *Merde alors.* It's all quite silly, in my view. We love God, we act with love, tolerance, respect, and honesty towards others, and that is all!

But I do understand the problem. It is terrifically difficult to detach oneself from one's origins, from all the stamped-in traditions, from all the constraints, in a word, that are imposed on us from our very first cry of anguish as we enter this world. It seems to me that each person's duty is to work towards her own liberation. It is only then that we'll really be able to discover ourselves, only then that we'll be able to blossom into who we really are, freed from all that deforms, pains, or destroys the soul.

Michel and Adeline did not come by to go out to the movies. So much the better (but I still feel irritated with them). I was able to see Rabia and write two letters, one to my old French teacher.

22 May
10:30   I've recently conceived a theory, with the help of a remark from Lily. It is the following. If there exists a sort of determinism in life, it is merely the reflection of one's own character. That is to say, if you regularly have the same sorts of experiences, if you seem to find yourself involved always with the same people but under different names, if your problems are always of more or less the same nature—frustration in love, lack of confidence in yourself, whatever—all this is not owing to the meddling of some cranky Greek god or other outside force but rather to *yourself,* your ways of facing and engaging people and the world. If you want this repetitive context of your life to change, then firstly you must change yourself!

22:15   A very tedious Sunday, despite all my efforts to enliven it. Had lunch with Rab at the Cité. She is still depressed because of Friday's experience, and she was not consolable today. Then I went to a so-so Renaissance music concert, and later invited Jean-Claude for tea. I'm finally getting down to some work, with the questionnaires.

23:55   Feeling better after some work, with more thoughts on chance and determinism.   It is undeniable that in the life of each one of us, determinism plays an important role.   I do not count heredity as a factor in determinism, or at least I feel it is of very little significance. Environment is the key.   You are born into a particular environment and social milieu, having had absolutely no choice in the matter, and there you will stay for about twenty years.   That is a terrifically long time, and you will necessarily be deeply influenced by your experiences during this period of life.   As you reach adulthood and start to pursue your dreams and a career, various surprising things will happen to you.   Are they really by chance?   This is my question.   Yes and no. Sometimes I think they really are.   But the more I ponder, the more it seems to me that no, not really, because by our nature, our character, we *place ourselves* in situations where such seemingly unexpected incidents can happen.   Our *character* is what is already determined, rather let's say formed, by our environment.   Thus it is our character that will determine the vast majority of events that will befall us in our life, with a very small number of these events being actually due to chance.

The problem that consequently presents itself is: How can one form one's own character?   It seems to me that as we have very few choices during the first eighteen years of our life, this task is very difficult.   How to alter the effects of eighteen or twenty years of experience lived precisely during the most crucial and impressionable period of life?

The short answer must be: with knowledge and insight, and with a massive effort.

37: So eager to be away!
23 May

11:00   I'm feeling itchy to be back in the USA—strange but happy sensation, never thought I'd feel this way.

23:45   People furnish nothing but disappointment. *To hell with everyone!* I made a special trip to the Cité to see Christine, who had left me a note this afternoon, but when I arrived, she was not there.

Tense day: insistent telegrams and notes from Reid Hall to call my father. I did so at three-fifteen. Arranged, the Spanish affair. I will meet Max at Madrid airport on June 21 at eight p.m.

Rent: I created a little scene when Madame Rameau asked me to pay a full month's rent although I will be staying only one week. My argument was realistic: who needs the money more: a well-established upper-middle-class family, or I, a poor student with a year's more study to do? She agreed to half a month's rent and so I paid only 150F.

I am working like an ox to prepare for exams and finish my projects on the *lycéens* and on Renaissance humanist thinkers.

24 May

9:15   Another damned strike, says my neighbor, but I've not yet gone down to see. *I am living in order to travel!* Just now I was planning my summer trips, and I'm very excited. This summer is going to be marvelous. I am going to hitchhike and then later buy an Interrail pass, either in Freiburg or in Berne.

14:45   We often say, "What a pity that you're leaving! It's only now that you've finally gotten used to things here!" But we are mistaken. On the contrary, it is exactly the time to leave when we start to consider everything "normal," when our routine begins to become regular, when life begins to become too automatic and too easy. Life should always include elements of struggle and surprise, without which the human being ceases to develop.

22:00 Magnificent! Spectacular! A storm has just passed over with thunder, lightning, and heavy pounding rain. I love violent weather. I study very efficiently in such conditions.

25 May

13:00   Took a history exam this morning. I took the same exam as the French students—despite having spoken with the prof, who had said I would be given a special topic, owing to my entry mid-year into the course—what an ass he is. But fortunately I think I wrote a good response to the question, a political question yet. I am much more interested in the Reformation, humanism, and the system of education of the time, and so I am rather proud to have been able to answer his question.

Nevertheless, there is no doubt at all that the quality of the course and of the teaching were starkly inferior to what you find back home.

Much more still to do—back to work!

22:20 I drank too much whiskey and orange juice and then I ate too much. Damnation to the man who forgets the indelible fact that he is *alone*. It is not in my destiny to have relationships that last. Adeline and Michel don't like me at all, and I haven't a friend in the world, a true friend. Well, perhaps one, Lily.

The subject here is the Brittany reunion. I would like to cry out that I don't give a damn about people—*I don't give a damn!*—but it wouldn't be true. I want only to be on the road once more. I'll hitchhike from Belgium to Spain, passing, I hope, through Pau. I'll sleep in the fields. I'll eat bread, cheese, and fruit. Just give me my freedom! At least I'll have my freedom.

People disappoint me and work, although stimulating, weighs me down. I am exhausted to the marrow of my bones. I have noticed that I refuse to change myself for people.

It is raining, fortunately. I like the sound of rain as I'm falling asleep. I need to sleep. I need to escape from this horrid evening past.

26 May

9:15 Nothing has changed! No friends, tomato on a stalk, all my work still to finish. I am sick of my life.

11:15 An hour ago crushed by the feeling of mediocrity and failure, I am now the victor! Thota, an artist friend, gave me a tiny Indian elephant and showed me his exposition. I bought bread for 1F and the girl gave me back five 20-centime pieces. (Perhaps she glanced at my emaciated face and did that on purpose.) But above all, the sun is shining and I realize that it is not wise to let oneself be perturbed by insignificant things. Life is too short for that, especially since I am waiting with exquisite impatience only to *leave*. To each one his road.

All I want is, firstly, the time to work; secondly, that people will be on time and keep their word (extremely important); thirdly, that people will be kind to me, even those who do not know me (shopkeepers, clerks); fourthly, that the weather will always be robust, that is, sunny, or stormy, or displaying a magnificent, cumulusly baroque sky, but none of this grey, weak, and indecisive stuff; finally, that I will be permitted total *freedom* in my life—freedom from slimy street *dragueurs*, from idiotic rules, from hunger, and with the means to buy books and travel to the farthest ends of the world.

27 May

1:00 Tonight—last night—I went out with Fleur, Eira (Pierre's Welsh girlfriend), and Rabia. They all came here to the bird's nest, and then we went to a very good Greek restaurant in the rue Mouffetard with live Greek music. Rabia went home after dinner, and the rest of us went to a pub on the rue de l'Ancienne Comédie. Ginger beer for me. Conversation with some Israelis.

Fun, superficially, but without substance. What can you ever say of any real significance when you're with a group? Why do so many people suddenly turn so dull when they converse as a group? Myself: I shock people because I am most often animated and enthusiastic. People find me an exaggeration. The Brittany group—notably Michel and Adeline—I think thought the same. But around people without passion, without inner fire, I die. They're as boring as drizzling rain.

At least I've had a good meal, and the weather in Paris is splendid right now.

My worst character fault is that I am a perfectionist without the drive to actually attain perfection. This seems tragic, and yet most the time I pass over it. I enjoy myself and in fact desire only to be a stroller through the streets, a leafer through books, an irresponsible bohemian. But one should not be stupid. One should not be disappointed in oneself either.

8:30 What splendid weather! A radiant sun and crystal skies! Did I mention that I took my theater exam yesterday and that it went very well? I wrote, I think, a very good essay on illusion in the theater

187

of Jean Genet using *Les bonnes* as an example. I find the play to be very existentialist: the theme is primarily the domination of people by other people. This play fascinates me!

14:00 Arranged! Paris—Strasbourg—Freiburg. Interrail Pass at Freiburg. Then Switzerland—Pau—Spain. Perfect!

21:00 A sudden insight: one must not attach too much importance to anything in this life, never to the point of becoming obsessed, maniacal, *complexé* over it. What I mean is, it is very dangerous to consider things or even very important people as sacrosanct, for in so doing you risk destroying the thing or the person, and secondly, you risk destroying yourself. I know that this is true.

It is curious how late night falls these days: ten minutes past nine and still a pastel-blue sky. I am not especially fond of this situation.

22:30 I find that my paper on politically-minded humanists of the Renaissance is going very well and that for once, I am going to produce a good piece of work. The French, despite their exaggeration of the thing, are not completely off the mark when they insist upon a good plan, good *form*.

38: Horrid green flies and something beyond chance

28 May

8:25   Everything is psychological. Nothing is a shock if you prepare well in advance to confront it.

22:30   I was working along quite well there—and God knows I have enough work to do right now— when I became aware that I had been invaded by hundreds of little green flying insects. *Merde!* I went down to Alice, and we came back with a cigarette and a sponge. I tried to continue working on Erasmus and the idea of the state, but when those little beasts would land on my papers and make dry little noises inside the lampshade, they set my nerves on edge!

Damn it all! I give up for the night.

It is only the most absurd things that happen to me in this blessed city: swarms of green flies in the middle of Paris! How is this possible? Is this some judgment from the gods? Or is Paris simply a mad, mad, mad, mad place?

Ten more days and I'm out of here. *With a big smile.*

29 May

7:20   Good morning. The Sorbonne bell tower never ceases to remind me of the hour.

15:50 Perturbed over Machiavelli, whose thoughts do not fit in neatly to the outline I've sketched for my paper!

Subjects for future reflection:

- The value of human effort entirely consecrated to one thing, as opposed to this same effort divided among several things.

- Does life have value if one spends one's time producing things that are only half done?

These and the question of determinism (although I have managed lately to understand this a bit better) plague my mind! I cannot spare the time to think about these subjects right now, but I *must* resolve them.

By the way, I detest man's intrinsic weakness. I also detest the fact that there is no objectivity in the world. I want ABSOLUTES!

30 May
2:10 I'm excited! I worked all day and all evening, and now I have the outline for my history paper on various philosophers of the Renaissance. I am even a bit afraid of it: the outline is sixteen pages long! But it is really quite good so far. I will need to work nonstop all week, that's the only problem, for I still have twenty-two questionnaires to analyze. I would like to have everything finished by June 3.

31 May

0:45   If I finish all my work, it will be a miracle. I helped Monica with her English tonight for the second time.

A couple of comments:

- It is better to know one thing thoroughly and correctly than to know many things only moderately.

- Those who respond to questions with many words are precisely those who know their subject least. One must always express the core of the matter and not rant on with superfluous details.

Et moi: I slog on with work and not much else except the occasional walk to clear my head.

15:40   Incredible, what I managed to do today. Got up at eight. Ate. Did laundry. Took a bath *chez* Rameau. Went to Gibert for paper. Took the subway to Opéra and the American Express office to pick up money Dad sent. Took bus back to Luxembourg. Went to BIGE office and bought my ticket to Freiburg via Strasbourg. Ate lunch at twelve-fifteen at Assas. Stopped in to Reid Hall to get mail and leave note for one of the directors, Phil. Took subway to the Gare de l'Est. Got schedule for Freiburg to Pau, going via Geneva and Marseilles. Subway to Saint-Michel. Post office and quick call to Phil. He will grade my *lycéen* project, which I will hand in on June 6. Bank: 200F. Pastry shop: *flan*. Back home: coffee, *flan*, and five minutes of repose with a wet cloth across my eyes, and then Christine came by! After fifteen minutes I had to show her the door, unfortunately, because I absolutely had to get to work. At least we chatted for a bit. To work!

1 June
1:25 I've worked constantly, except for an hour's dinner break and later a short tea break, and—announcement!—I have a dissertation of forty pages! And it's good! My head feels like a pumpkin. Tomorrow I'll have to recopy it.

2 June
0:45 I am going to kill myself if I keep up this pace. I have never worked so hard in my life.

Got a 13 on my history exam—quite good! But he is still an idiot, that prof.

Worked on questionnaires, *bac A.* Lunch at Concordia. Montmartre: I had to take a walk there before leaving Paris, and the weather was splendid. Worked four to six-thirty. Dinner at Concordia. Worked from seven-thirty until half past midnight.

I feel I've caught a bit of a cold. Six hours of sleep a night for a whole week is not wise. But no help for it.

12:50 I cannot believe it. In one week I have assembled a forty-two-page dissertation in Renaissance history that is absolutely brilliant! I tell you, I am flabbergasted in front of it—the miracle that it is *there*, and the quality of the work. I don't believe myself.

17:15   Finally! Do you know what I have learned this   year?   TOTAL   INDEPENDENCE. Intellectually, for all semester I was working solely for myself, not for the profs, and I'm very happy with the results. And personally, for I've done what I want, when I want, and no one has constrained me. It is actually quite remarkable how much confidence I've gained in myself these past four months since arriving in Paris.

But back to work, for I still have one last job to do: finish analyzing the *lycéen* survey. *Allez, hop!*

23:15   This must be it, I am terribly sorry, but I do believe in it, in something beyond mere chance: in *divine intervention* in certain cases! This evening I went to the good-bye party for the Americans. It was at a charming little bistro on the rue Greneta in the second *arrondissement;* I'll speak later about the gathering. To come home, I walked just down to the Ile de la Cité, where I felt like catching a bus. At the Saint-Michel stop, I glanced outside at the people who were awaiting the bus. And there was Michel, who boarded and came to sit next to me! We chatted, and he is going to stop by to see me tomorrow afternoon.

Blessed "chance"! There *is* something beyond chance, all the same, and beyond determinism based on our character—yes, there is. Although by our character we create what happens to ourselves most of the time, at certain other times truly strange and coincidental events confront us, bizarre incidents which seem to come out of the blue and touch our hearts, and I, for one, cannot now but ask myself whether God is not actively planning things out for us.

Dear Michel! I had completely renounced his friendship after that evening when he and Adeline failed to come by as planned, and my decision was reinforced after the Brittany reunion. I also began to attack my studies like a wage-earning coal miner, thinking that I had already lost too much valuable time on worthless socializing. I still liked Michel very much but felt the right thing to do must be to renounce any pursuit of his friendship. And suddenly there he was, right next to me on the bus! When you consider such seemingly coincidental and serendipitous incidents, could the hand of God really be at work? If I had left the restaurant later or earlier, if I had not stopped to ask directions to the *métro* from a man in the rue Saint-Denis, if I had chosen to walk home rather than take the bus... There are—it seems there *must be*—things in our life that are pre-planned for us. It seems Michel is meant to stay in my life for at least a while longer!

As for the party. Excellent food. Fellow student David confided to me his personal chronicle of the Paris experience. Anne has the same attitude as ever towards me. Anne! That girl escapes me, I must admit. Usually I understand people quite well, but she remains a closed book. It seems that she admires me a lot but that I make her very ill-at-ease. She said she'd like to see me before we all disperse. We will meet for dinner Monday night. Anne seems to need a lot of security in her life, she is extremely sensitive (even excessively), and she has the tendency to worry far too much.

Paris. Coming home tonight amidst the sparkling lights and gaiety of the city in springtime, I thought, *Good Lord, all the same, Paris, you are not my city. You are still a mystery to me. You are still as overwhelming as you were to me my first weeks here. You are still vast, and a lonely place, and Paris, old beauty, I cannot stay with you. I have survived the experience of living in you for four months, but in the end, you are not my city and we must part.*

39: *Confidence at last!*
3 June
7:15   Ah Jacques Brel. Without at all knowing his personal history, I will guess that he had a significant love affair in Paris, and that he was very disappointed by a too-religious Belgian lover. I had dreams of love last night.

10:10   I am beginning the moving-out process. I am going to withdraw all my money in the form of travelers checks, and later I am going to send away some packages. I am packing my suitcase. This is anguishing. Leaving always involves some kind of anguish. Departures, trips—these are exciting. But completely terminating something we've come to know—in this case, my relationship with Paris—produces a feeling of being between two worlds, of landing in "the twilight zone," on the point of the total unknown.

22:30   One cannot deny that I am quite courageous, for I am. Everything is in order. Unable to buy travelers checks in francs, I will carry with me in cash 1531F (= $300). I'll be careful. Mailed a box of books home; the rest will go Monday. The big suitcase is also ready and will go Monday. Telephoned Strasbourg and booked a hotel room. Will travel overnight and arrive Wednesday the 8th early in the morning.

Michel came by to see me, and this boy is terrific. We talked again for a long time in my room, and we have promised to write to each other. Dinner with Rabia at the Cité. The dining room at the International House is infernal, the noise terrible. Letter from Lily! She writes that she plans to spend most of June in Switzerland and would like to meet me, but I fear it is too late to make such arrangements.

To work. It is hard to have to work when you have a thousand other things in your head.

4 June
7:15 Ah, the anguish has fled. Much better! Now I am excited and full of hope. In this world it is very important to know when you should listen to people and when, on the contrary, you shouldn't. Each is indispensable; the trick is exercising good judgment.

23:30   Everything, bit by bit, is getting done and wrapped up. The *lycéen* survey report will be complete by tomorrow morning. Letter to Lily suggesting we meet in Berne. But I doubt this will work. These last-minute attempts to arrange *rendez-vous* at great distance never work out.

Ran out of *resto-u* tickets. So much the better—I was sick of all that. Nevertheless, those chow-downs were a good bargain.

I can fool almost everyone now with my French. At least no one ever guesses that I'm American. But what is still lacking with this language is the possibility of expressing the most subtle nuances. There I must admit that I am stronger in English—normal. But it is completely the case now that I think and formulate my ideas in French, not in English, and this for quite a while, almost since last November in Pau. It will be peculiar to change back to English when I return to the USA, painful and difficult at times, too, I think.

I must return once more to the Louvre before I leave. And I want to see a good French film, too, perhaps *La Communion solennelle*.

Remark: Anne is egotistical. Another remark: So is the whole world. One must not worry about this but simply continue one's path of happiness.

5 June
7:20   Why did I get up so early this morning? When in addition I knew I'd fallen ill, numbskull

that I am. Yes, it's rotten but true: I have a cold, *merde*. Too many Camembert sandwiches, too many long hours of work on the dissertation, and not enough sleep. Funny, therefore, that I should arise so early. I will finish the report, then I will try to nap. If it is sunny and warm today, I will go install myself on a chair in the Jardin du Luxembourg.

23:59   I can't believe it! I've just finished my *lycéen* survey report and it's brilliant! It's spectacular! It's one hundred pages plus the notes on Vincent and Minot. It's got a fantastic introduction, a brilliant concluding analysis, and I'm so damn proud of myself I could shout! I did the whole blasted thing on my own with no academic advising whatsoever. It's a masterpiece. It's fabulous.

This is it—I've got it—I've obtained, at last, CONFIDENCE in myself!

40: More encounters on the brink of departure
6 June
17:30   Finally, a normal day. It is good to regain my old habits after being separated from them for a week due to grueling work. Packages of books sent by post. Suitcase sent by SERNAM—had to take a taxi to get there. Then, carefree and full of joy, I went for one last visit to the Louvre. Rubens room—extraordinary. A peek at some Italian and Dutch paintings of the seventeenth century, another look at the French, and a glide by some

Greek sculptures, of course the Venus de Milo. Farewell, lovely Louvre.

Afterwards in the street I was chatted up by a Frenchman, whom I allowed to walk alongside me since he did not seem dangerous. We went for a drink in a café across from the Louvre. I must note that this was the first time that I had been pursued by a native Parisian, an electrical engineer who lives in the rich western suburbs yet! He said that when he saw me coming out of the Louvre, I had such a happy smile on my face. (Didn't Agon say the same, so many weeks ago?) He wanted to see me again, said he enjoyed hikes in the country, and I would have liked this, but luck was not on our side, since I am all set to depart tomorrow. He was open, likeable, quite sweet. He gave me his work address in Paris so that if I am ever again passing through, we can see each other.

Truly, sometimes good things arrive too late. It would have been really nice to have had a male French friend with whom to go on hikes in the hills, and to see from time to time in Paris. Well, *c'est la vie*.

Later, walking towards the Place des Vosges, I stopped at Beaubourg to listen to records, for I'd always wanted to do that. And there while standing in line, I met another Frenchman, a slim young man of twenty-four who began to speak to me first. *(Décidément,* where were all these attractive Frenchmen all these months?) We ended up sitting next to each other and listening raptly to the same record, Serge Reggiani. Gilles was a photographer, had studied letters and philosophy briefly, then had dropped them. He was repulsed by Paris but was here because of his studies and because of the fact that he was born here. A fascinating man because rather mad, eccentric, and he made me laugh—it is rare for me to laugh so much.

After we'd listened to music and I'd bought a Chagall postcard, he and I walked out together. Yes, he was repulsed by Paris because the people were not friendly, the lifestyle ugly and noisy. His Gauloises revolted him, too, but he smoked them because he did not have enough money to buy Marlboros. "You cannot imagine how very much America influences France." He kept dropping his little franc as we walked. He had a way of walking that was completely focus-less, as if he were not really there.

I felt like seeing the Place des Vosges, so we headed there together. An extraordinary person, this Gilles. He told me his story, more or less, as we walked and later as we sat on a bench at the Place. He's from a respectable middle-class family, and a fairly conservative one. He, however, is of a leftist temperament. He became sick of the comfortable life and at age nineteen after his *bac A*, he left home. He became a true leftist and began to work for *Libération,* a radical French newspaper. This obviously did not go down at all well with the very rightist mentality of his father, and *voilà* a falling-out. When he decided to study letters, his father grudgingly approved although he would have preferred his son choose law. But when he abandoned letters for photography, that was the last straw! A conflict of temperament, of taste, perhaps of values. It's a crying shame that some parents believe themselves to be the masters of their children's lives.

We took the bus together towards Saint-Michel, and he continued to tell me his story. Gilles now lives near the rue Mouffetard in an apartment with his girlfriend and two other couples. We walked up the boulevard together, and I can attest that it was the most pleasant walk along the old Boul' Mich that I have had since my arrival in Paris. How he made me laugh! What a wonderful character he was! I treated him to a hamburger and a coke at McDonald's because he was hungry. He ate very quickly, and we exchanged addresses, for I would really like to write to him. He did not thank me for the snack, but this did not bother me at all for some reason. After this, he had to go, having an appointment to keep, and so did I. He sent me a kiss in the air.

23:20 What a long, full day! At seven-thirty, Anne and I met in front of my building, and we went to dine at a good little Indian restaurant where we ate beef and chicken curry, drank good cider (which after a while made me a bit drunk), and discussed our feelings about having lived in France for the past nine months. We admitted that Pau and Paris were two completely different adventures and that Paris was definitely the harder of the two. But personally, I said, Paris had taught me more than

Pau with regard to independence and the art of managing my life. She agreed, and we were both a bit afraid of returning to the USA. Why? Two reasons, each intertwined with the other: we don't want to fall back into the same more or less comfortable, banal life next year; and, having better discovered our deepest self, we want to be able to affirm our personality around friends and family who perhaps will not understand the changes in us right away.

I have to confess that I am actually rather proud of how I've dealt with this Parisian experience. Confronted at the beginning with a frightening, overwhelming city, with very disappointing professors, and with the most absolute solitude that I have ever known, I succeeded in getting used to Paris, in doing excellent work, in finding friends, and in developing the capacity, when friends were unavailable, to support my solitude without anguish. Anguished morning awakenings disappeared.

Towards the end of our meal we were telling each other little stories about the daily inconveniences of life in Paris, and Anne voiced the common complaint of not being able to get change for the pay phone.

The store clerk: "I have nothing to do with the telephone on the corner."

Anne sighed, "I resigned myself to the fact that making a phone call takes at least two hours. 'Let's see, I'll study in the morning, and in the afternoon I'll make a phone call.'"

I laughed and laughed. And the two gentlemen next to us smiled and began to talk with us. That was pleasant, and they were Bretons, what good luck! We chatted with them for about thirty minutes.

After leaving the Indian restaurant, Anne and I sought out dessert a few doors down at a little Italian café. We sat at the bar and ordered ice cream, and we chatted with the friendly, handsome Italian waiters, who were very likeable.

After this boisterous evening, I bid Anne good-bye. She still had a paper to write before her departure on Friday. We'll meet again in August, back at the university.

41: Farewell! Yet all remains to be seen
7 June
20:00 I am writing at the Gare de l'Est. Rabia and I met for lunch earlier at the Café Le Luxembourg, where we talked and laughed and I recounted to her my latest adventures. She is thinking about going to America this year in August, and we hope to be able to see each other. She is still with her French *amant* and they are starting to talk of getting married! I was overjoyed for her. "I haven't told my parents yet," she said.

When I returned to my room at three, I lay down on the bed and promptly fell asleep for two hours. I woke up with a start at about five and looked around the old hole. Everything had been sent or packed up. All was bare once more, clinic-white, the Italian wine bottle the only item adorning the shelves, the varnished card table cleared except for my purse, a small backpack, and a snack. Had I really lived and worked here these past four months? Struggled, raged, cried, laughed? At that moment it all felt like a dream from which I was just waking up.

At six p.m. my dear old Agon came by to see me. I had telephoned him yesterday to let him know of my departure and, no longer nervous or afraid, invited him for coffee in my room. I met him at the massive front door of my building, where we were all smiles, and we then climbed the steep grey service stairs together to my room. In fact there was no coffee to be had, as I had given it and the camping-gas to Patrice. But I had bought little bottles of pineapple juice and had half a packet still of Breton butter biscuits, which we enjoyed. Agon sat on my bed while I sat in my study chair. Diverse misunderstandings had separated us, notably that time at Censier when we had espied each other but had said nothing. In any case, we sorted everything out and no hard feelings remained. We forgave each other. He understood that I had to return to the USA to finish my bachelor's degree. Sitting across from him, listening to him, gazing into his sensitive eyes for perhaps the last time, I thought silently to myself that Agon truly was a very good man, a gentle soul.

It was time to go. I grabbed my purse and small traveling bag and we went down to the boulevard, where he bought a book bag. I looked for a good paperback for the trip but didn't find one. As he walked with me towards the *métro*, the moment of parting approaching, Agon did not spell out what he'd said a few weeks before, but his intention was clear, very clear: he would like to marry me. We said we would write to each other and see how things went. Perhaps it was only the natural effect of parting, or perhaps his faithful steadfastness touched me, but I suddenly felt a pang of real fondness for this man. But I heard myself say that if he found someone else he shouldn't hesitate, he shouldn't wait for me. He looked at me intensely as I said this, stoically perhaps, and remained silent. Again I felt affection for him and a nudge of uncertainty—was I really making the right decision here?—and I assured him yes, we will write to each other and see.

But now, my train for Strasbourg has just announced boarding!

Candid reader comments about this work are very welcome: do let us know your thoughts! Go to *Paris Broke Me (In)* on Amazon and write a customer review. ⊗

Made in the USA
Monee, IL
08 January 2020